The Curious BOY'S Book of Adventure

The Curious BOY'S Book of Adventure

Sam Martin

BLOOMSBURY

First published in Great Britain in 2007 by Bloomsbury Publishing Plc,
36 Soho Square, London, W1D 3QY

Copyright © 2007 Elwin Street Limited

Conceived and produced by
Elwin Street Limited
144 Liverpool Road
London N1 1LA
United Kingdom
www.elwinstreet.com

A CIP catalogue record of this book is available from the British Library

ISBN 978 07475 9512 0

1 3 5 7 9 10 8 6 4 2

Cover illustration: Tony Palmer
Internal design: Thomas Keenes
Illustrations: David Eaton
Animal tracks (page 53) reprinted by kind permission of
the Massachusetts Division of Fisheries and Wildlife

Printed in China

This book is dedicated to my two sons Ford and Wren
—may your own adventures be long and bright.

The completion of this book would not have been possible without the support and guidance of a number of people. My loving and wise wife Denise deserves most of the thanks, both for her encouragement and tireless work pursuing her own career while keeping our family in shoes and sandwiches. I'd also like to thank my editor Dan Mills for his understanding and direction. Lastly, a hearty shout out to my two research assistants Jason Miller and Jerry Fugit, whose deft skills of investigation helped shed light on many a complicated subject. I hope all those who are young and young at heart can find the inspiration in these pages to live their own adventurous lives.

Contents

Chapter 4 – Building 98

Chapter 5 – Fun! 124

Index 158

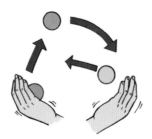

Introduction

✦✦✦

TO SAY THAT BOYS OF ALL AGES LIKE TO HUNT, EXPLORE and build things is quite an understatement. Truth be told, we can't help ourselves. Show any boy – aged from seven to 70 – a trail that disappears off into a wood, or a Bunsen burner next to some empty beakers, and his imagination will automatically start running like a finely tuned sports car. Say the word 'treehouse', and boys everywhere will begin gathering water balloons; mention an expedition and our minds immediately turn to Everest and the North Pole. Adventure is in our DNA.

The problem is that a lot of us are having trouble getting in touch with our adventurous DNA – the part of our nature that, 50 years ago, would have seen a giant oak tree, a sheet of plywood and a rope and known just what to do. Our adventuring instincts have been dulled over the years by video games, television and all those electronic toys that short-circuit the imagination. These days, a boy might think 'a message in a bottle' is a new e-mail programme, and 'tracking a wild animal' is a new instant messaging feature. Some of us couldn't climb a tree or skim a stone if our portable music players depended on it.

But it's not our fault – many of us simply don't know what we're missing. After all, lots of the experiments, projects, hunts and explorations in this book date back to a bygone age, a time when fishing rods and bows and arrows were as important to a boy as a set of spurs to a cowboy on a cattle drive.

Back before computers and television started dulling those after-school hours, there was real adventure in the fresh air of the great outdoors, and you didn't need a sea voyage or a jungle expedition to find it. The good news is, it's still there! You just need to know where to start.

Whether you're a curious kid, or a grown-up boy looking to recapture your own childhood adventures, you've picked up the right book. The lost world of fun and hijinks may have been pushed aside by video games and computers, but that doesn't mean it no longer exists. Our adventurous DNA might have been put to sleep by a lack of use, but all you have to do to wake it up is open the back door. Adventure and excitement are out there, for anyone who's curious.

How to use this book

Some adventures are more difficult than others, and you might want a few extra hands to help out. Every activity is graded for difficulty by the number of symbols underneath the title.

One-symbol projects are for solo adventurers. Two-symbol projects might take a little more time and need someone else to help out. Three-symbol projects are serious adventures.

⚠ Projects marked with this symbol involve tools, fire, or other elements that can be dangerous. Always make sure an adult knows what you're doing and is around to help out with these tasks.

Chapter One

Exploring

WHAT'S THE BEST WAY TO FIND SOME ADVENTURE?
Get out into the great outdoors and do some
exploring. Go for a hike in the woods, build a
treehouse; you can have some great adventures
learning how to tie knots, or practising your
Morse Code for those secret spy missions ahead.

✦

Then at night there's an entire universe overhead
to search for planets and constellations of Greek
gods and goddesses. OK, the great explorers of
the past sailed for the South Pole or tramped
through Africa, but all those men had to start
somewhere. Perhaps it was by taking a
running leap out the back door.

Tying knots

❧ ❧

No one should set off for a day of adventure without knowing how to tie a few good knots. You can use knots to tie logs together to make a raft, or to string up a home-made tent in case of sudden rainstorms. If you ever want to try sailing or mountain climbing, knowing how to tie these knots will give you a head start.

DID YOU KNOW? In the past, knots have been used as home-made calculators. The Inca people in Peru would put knots in long pieces of string to keep track of village populations, food stores, trade and to calculate taxes. Even though the Incas were without a written language, these knotted strings – known as *quipu* – helped them calculate and record the data needed to run an empire.

YOU WILL NEED

● String or rope

REEF KNOT

1 A REEF KNOT IS EASY TO TIE, and can be used in most situations. It's also easy to loosen: just push one end towards the knot. Using two ropes, make an 'X' left over right, and then bring one end through the loop as if you're tying your shoelaces.

2 REPEAT THIS PROCESS, but this time make the 'X' right over left. Pull it tight, and you will have the knot.

BOWLINE

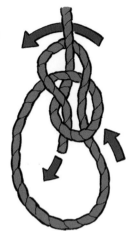

1 ROCK CLIMBERS USE THE BOWLINE because it forms a quick non-slipping loop – perfect for attaching yourself to a climbing buddy as you scale the side of a mountain or climb your favourite tree. It's known by some as 'the king of knots'. Begin by making a loop in one end of the rope.

2 THEN TAKE THE OTHER END UP THROUGH the loop, around the rope on the other side, and back where it came from.

3 IN THE SCOUTS, THEY USED TO TEACH IT to young'uns with the old 'rabbit story': the rabbit comes up through the hole, round the tree, and back down the hole again.

CLOVE HITCH

1 THE CLOVE HITCH IS THE BEST knot to use when lashing two logs or pieces of wood together, to make a raft or treehouse. Not only is it easy on the rope, but because the rope crosses over on itself the knot actually gets stronger the harder you pull on it. Make this knot by looping the rope over the log. Pass the end of the rope over and across itself and around the wood again.

2 THEN FEED THE END UNDER the rope crossing the top, so that it comes out in the opposite direction to the rest of the rope.

TIMBER HITCH

1 **IF YOU FIND SOMETHING BIG** in the woods
and want to drag it home you'll need to
know the timber hitch. This is the knot
that lumberjacks used to tie around
fallen tree trunks to drag the timber to
the saw mill.

2 **LOOP YOUR ROPE AROUND A LOG** and
bring the short end up and around the long
end of the rope. Bring the short end back down
through the loop from the direction in which it
came. Bring it over and under itself two or three
times. When the long end is pulled, the knot tightens onto itself.

SHEET BEND

1 **IN SITUATIONS WHERE YOU NEED** to tie the
end of a small rope to the end of a large rope,
this is the knot to use. It's called a sheet bend
because sailors used it to 'bend the sheets' or
tie the ropes in the rigging of a ship. This
could come in handy if you're ever stranded
on a desert island and need to rig a sail.

2 **FORM A LOOP WITH THE LARGER ROPE.**
Thread the smaller rope through the loop, and
bring one end around the neck of the larger
rope's loop.

3 **BRING THE SMALL ROPE BACK** under itself but
don't go back through the loop. Pull tight.

Splicing a rope

If you have two small ropes and you need one long one, you can splice the ends together. This will give you a much stronger rope than just tying the two together with a knot. One type of splice is an eye splice, in which a loop is made in the end of one rope by splicing it into itself. A more common splice is the end-to-end splice, also known as a short splice. This project will take about an hour.

YOU WILL NEED

- A marlin-spike: an old sailor's tool found on penknives that's used to open up the end of the rope
- A penknife
- Two pieces of three-strand rope

STEPS

1 LOOSEN AND UNWIND the ends of both ropes to a length of 25 cm (10 in) by pushing the tip of the marlin-spike into the end of the rope and peeling each strand back.

2 MATCH EACH STRAND with a corresponding strand on the opposite rope. It can be helpful to put coloured tape on each pair of strands to help you keep track.

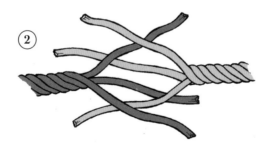

3 NOW COMES THE TRICKY PART: using your marlin-spike, pull out a loop of one strand from the part of the rope that's still twisted, and tuck the corresponding strand from the other rope through it. Pull it tight, and repeat the process with the other pairs of strands, always making sure to weave the same two corresponding strands together.

4 ONCE ALL SIX ENDS have been tucked under a loop, go back to the first strand and pull out a loop of rope from the next turn below your first weaving. Tuck the end of the corresponding strand under it as before, and do the same with the other ends.

5 KEEP WORKING DOWN the rope, tucking the ends under loops of the opposite strand, until at least 15 cm (6 in) of rope has been woven together.

6 ONCE YOU'RE HAPPY with the length of rope you've spliced together, cut off the loose ends to leave everything shipshape.

7 REMEMBER THAT SPLICING TWO ROPES together in this manner will cause the spliced section to be thicker than the original rope, which may cause trouble if you're feeding the rope through a small hole or ring.

Signalling

Some forms of long-distance signalling – like messages in a bottle and smoke signals – have been around for ages. And since the 1800s, more complex signalling systems have been invented to allow us to send complicated messages across great distances.

Sending a message in a bottle

When you think of a message in a bottle, you might think of a castaway like Robinson Crusoe desperately trying to find a way to get off his desert island. But sending messages by setting a bottle adrift in the ocean has actually been an important form of official communication. During the 1500s, the Royal Navy would float bottled messages to Queen Elizabeth I. It was a crime for anyone other than the Queen's official 'Uncorker of Ocean Bottles' to open a bottle with a message in it. Later, in the United States, Benjamin Franklin charted ocean currents by dropping bottles into the Gulf Stream. He found out where they went by including his address in the bottle. Whenever anyone found one of his messages, they would return it to him through the post.

YOU WILL NEED

- A thick glass bottle with a cork
- Wax
- Paper
- Ribbon
- A stapler or some glue
- A pencil

STEPS

1 WRITE A NOTE. Always write in pencil so it won't fade or smudge if it gets damp and be sure to put your name, date and address so whoever finds it can send you a note through the post. Write something about your home town or your hopes and dreams.

2 STAPLE OR GLUE A RIBBON to a corner of the note. Then roll up your note around the pencil.

3 HOLDING THE OTHER END OF THE RIBBON, drop your note and pencil into the bottle.

4 SECURE THE FREE END OF the ribbon to the bottom of your cork (again with glue or staples), and press the cork firmly into the bottle until it's snug.

> **WARNING**
>
> Make sure you set the bottle afloat when the tide is going out, so the bottle will go out to sea instead of ending up a few metres down the shore.

5 HEAT THE WAX IN A PAN. Once it has melted, dip the corked end of your bottle in to seal it.

6 TOSS THE BOTTLE INTO THE SEA or a fast-flowing river, and wait to see if anyone finds it and writes back to you.

Smoke signals

There is no smoke signal language so smoke signals are used only to send basic communications. The most common signal is a call for help or a warning of danger, which is three puffs of smoke. Signals for more complicated messages have to be planned out in advance between the sender and the recipient, which is more fun anyway. It's like having your own secret language! Sample messages might be one puff for 'attention' and two puffs for 'all's well'.

DID YOU KNOW? We all know that the Native Americans used smoke to communicate but did you know the Chinese did it too? The towers on the Great Wall of China were actually built in the 1600s as signalling stations, to send smoke signals along the Wall's entire 6350-km (3948-mile) length.

YOU WILL NEED

- A clear, high place
- A small, hot fire
- Pine needles, grass, wet wood chips or evergreen boughs
- A blanket or tarpaulin

STEPS

1 LIGHT YOUR CAMPFIRE (see page 59). Once the flames have died down into lots of hot burning coals, toss two or three handfuls of pine needles, fresh green grass or leaves, wet wood chips or evergreen boughs on the fire. These produce lots of smoke.

2 ONCE THE FIRE STARTS SMOKING, throw your blanket or tarpaulin over the top and then pull it off almost immediately. If there are two people involved, each should take one side of the blanket and hold it momentarily above the rising smoke before removing it. This should send 'puffs' of smoke up into the air that will be visible from all around.

WARNING

If you or your clothes ever catch fire you should stop what you're doing immediately, drop to the ground and put out the flames by rolling yourself backwards and forwards.

The semaphore code

Favoured by Scouts and Guides, the semaphore code uses hand-held flags or lights to signal messages between two people within sight of each other. Developed by the Frenchman Claude Chappe in 1794 using pivoted arms on a post, the relative positions of the two flags represent letters of the alphabet and numbers.

To signal that a transmission is beginning, the letters 'VOX' or 'VE' are signalled. The signaller then awaits a 'go-ahead' signal (usually the letter 'K') back from the receiver before continuing.

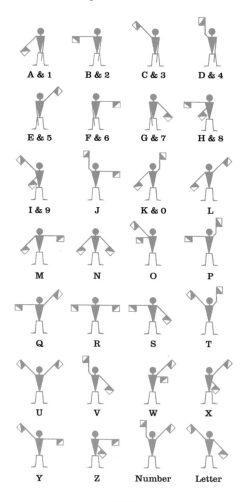

How to send a message in Morse Code

This code is recognised around the world. It's made up of dots and dashes that represent letters and numbers. These can be made by any means available – radio, horns, sirens, using a torch, blowing a whistle, banging on drums or even tapping on walls. A dash is three times the length of a dot. A space the length of a dot is left between symbols, two dots between letters and a dash between words.

A	•–	J	•–––	S	•••	1	•––––
B	–•••	K	–•–	T	–	2	••–––
C	–•–•	L	•–••	U	••–	3	•••––
D	–••	M	––	V	•••–	4	••••–
E	•	N	–•	W	•––	5	•••••
F	••–•	O	–––	X	–••–	6	–••••
G	––•	P	•––•	Y	–•––	7	––•••
H	••••	Q	––•–	Z	––••	8	–––••
I	••	R	•–•	0	–––––	9	––––•

•–•• • – ••• •– –•• •••– • –• – ••– •–• •

Morse Code was invented in 1838 by Samuel F. B. Morse, who was also the inventor of the telegraph. The telegraph transmits Morse Code as electric current down a wire. It comes out sounding like a series of clicks.

So how useful is it? Well, the infamous murderer Doctor Crippen was captured in 1910 thanks to Morse Code. Crippen murdered his wife in their London home, buried her body in the cellar and fled on a boat to Canada. The captain recognised him as one of his passengers from a police description, and telegraphed a message in Morse code to the authorities in London. The police caught up with him in Quebec, and he was hanged for his crime. The case was famous for being the first to be solved with the help of new radio technology.

The most famous Morse signal nowadays is the distress signal 'S O S' (short for 'save our souls'). If you hear this signal, you know someone needs help right away, and if you get in trouble and need a way to call for assistance, this is how to do it. At sea, this signal is only used in real emergencies, and in some places it's against the law to use it at any other time. The signal is:

•••–––•••

Building a bridge

Wide, full streams can scupper an expedition (or turn it into a wet one) unless you know how to get across carefully. Sometimes you can find a narrow, shallow area to cross by taking off your shoes and rolling up your trousers or by placing a few rocks to make stepping stones. When you just can't wade or step across, you can always build a simple log bridge.

> **DID YOU KNOW?** This simple type of bridge is only good for short distances, because there's nothing to support the middle of the span. Bigger bridges carrying heavier loads are always designed to support themselves in the middle so they don't collapse. Arch bridges, for example, are designed so that each stone rests on another one slightly below it. They were widely used by the Roman Empire. Suspension bridges use cables or ropes tied to each bank to hold up the middle. They were first used by the Incas in South America. Modern materials, like steel and concrete, are strong enough to build massive bridges: The world's longest suspension bridge is the Akashi-Kaikyo bridge in Japan, which is nearly 4,000 m (13,000 ft) long!

This is a project you're going to need some help on. You and your co-adventurers should be able to lift and secure a long log into place, and it shouldn't take more than an hour or so.

YOU WILL NEED

- A felled tree long enough to span the stream with at least half a metre of log on either bank, thick enough to support your weight
- A collection of medium-sized rocks
- A small axe (optional)

STEPS

1 **FIND THE NARROWEST SECTION OF THE STREAM.** This job is best done where the stream is no more than 3 m (10 ft) wide. Then locate a felled tree, at least 60 cm (2 ft) longer than the width of the stream, and drag it to the spot so that it's perpendicular to the stream (so it looks like a 'T'). The end closest to the stream should be about 30 cm (1 ft) away from the water.

WARNING

When tipping the log over, make sure you get a safe distance away when it starts to fall.

2 **GO TO THE END FARTHEST FROM THE WATER** and lift the log up. Then push it upright so that the log is standing up straight like a telegraph pole. This is the bit you might want help with – logs can be pretty heavy!

3 **IN THE SAME MOTION,** push the log over so that it falls across the stream and onto the far bank.

4 **PULL OR PUSH THE LOG** so that it sits on the bank an equal amount on both sides of the stream. You want a good footing for both ends of your bridge in case the bank crumbles when you stand on it.

5 **PILE AND STACK UP MEDIUM-SIZED ROCKS** and lots of soil on either side of the log to secure the near end in place on the stream bank.

6 **CAREFULLY WALK ACROSS THE LOG** and secure the opposite side of your bridge in the same way.

7 **TO MAKE YOUR LOG BRIDGE EVEN MORE SECURE,** you can notch smaller logs with an axe and place them underneath each end to hold it in place. Or you can anchor it with ropes tied to a tree on each bank.

8 **YOU CAN USE TWO LOGS SIDE-BY-SIDE** to make your bridge wider. And, if you like, you can flatten off the tops a little with an axe to make them easier to walk on.

Building a treehouse

✦✦✦

Building a treehouse is always a great adventure. Once you've finished, it'll make a great look-out platform, fort or base camp. Fit it with pulleys, climbing ropes and telescopes and you can spend hours exploring without even moving.

To build a treehouse you'll need to get a few friends in to help, and it's going to take some time. Start at the beginning of the summer when school finishes, and keep working on it bit by bit until it's completed. By the end of the summer it should look great.

Finding the right tree to build in is the key to a sturdy treehouse. Choose a tree that has a minimum of three branches that spread out equal distances from one side of the trunk. They should be at least 20 cm (8 in) thick to support the weight of you and a few friends.

There's always the temptation to build as high as you can, but you have to consider the wind. A treehouse platform acts just like a sail when it comes to the wind and things can sway around a lot, especially when you're up high. Better to aim for between 3 and 4.5 m (10 and 15 ft) off the ground. That'll still feel quite high enough when you're up there in a breeze!

YOU WILL NEED   ⚠

- A tree
- A sheet of 2-cm (1-in) thick ply-wood, 1.2 x 2.4 m (4 x 8 ft)
- Several lengths of wood, 5 x 10 cm (2 x 4 in)
- 5-cm (2-in) galvanised nails
- A hammer
- A saw
- A ladder
- Rope

STEPS

1 START BY CUTTING 45-cm (18-in) long pieces from your lengths of wood to make a basic ladder up the trunk of the tree. Pick the exact spot you want to build in, and work out how many rungs you'll need on your ladder to climb up to it.

2 ONCE THE LENGTHS HAVE BEEN CUT, use at least two nails set side-by-side in each piece to nail the rungs to the tree. Space them about 60 cm (2 ft) apart, leading up the trunk to the base of the branches where the platform of the treehouse will be secured.

3 HOW YOU ACCESS THE PLATFORM will depend on the shape of your tree. Most of the time, the ladder will come up right under the best branches for building on. That's fine: you'll just have to cut a hole in your floor to climb through. If you keep the piece of wood you cut out, you can use it to make a trap door.

4 NEXT, HAUL THE SHEET OF PLYWOOD into the tree and position it between the branches where you think it will be most sturdy.

5 MARK THE TREE LIMBS with a pencil or nail where the plywood touches them and lower the plywood back down.

6 CUT SEVERAL MORE 45-cm (18-in) long pieces of wood and nail them to the tree at the spots you've marked to act as blocks for your platform.

7 LIFT THE PLYWOOD carefully into place by having two people on the ground pass it up to two people in the tree. Nail the plywood to the blocks.

8 NEXT, MAKE RAILINGS by nailing up more lengths of plywood between the branches or by tying up lengths of rope to surround your platform.

9 FROM HERE YOU CAN ADD A TRAP DOOR, extra ladder steps leading to higher branches, and miniature seats or platforms on surrounding look-out points.

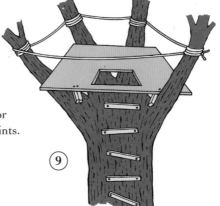

Making a tent

On the streets of Cairo, Egypt, you can still see the ancient art of tent-making as it was practised hundreds of years ago. Huge tent-pavilions known as *suradeq* are still being made in the city's old quarter. Largely hand-sewn, these palace-like tents can take several months to complete and are used for family gatherings and celebrations.

You won't need to make a tent that big – let's just focus on keeping the rain off you and your exploration team. Once you get the tent up, collect pine needles, dried leaves, grass and other soft things to make a natural floor. It shouldn't take more than an hour if you're working by yourself, faster if there's two of you.

YOU WILL NEED

- A 2.4- x 3.6-m (8- x 12-ft) tarpaulin with grommets (eye-holes) round the edges
- 7 m (24 ft) of rope
- At least four large rocks, stakes or sticks

STEPS

1 LOCATE TWO TREES about 3 m (10 ft) apart. These will act as the supports for your tent.

2 RUN YOUR ROPE through the centre grommet on each of the longer sides of the tarpaulin, bisecting it into 1.3- x 2.4-m (6- x 8-ft) rectangles.

3 ABOUT 1.5 M (5 FT) OFF THE GROUND, securely tie your rope to the trees you've selected. The point of tie-off should be roughly the same height on each tree. The tarpaulin should drape over this roof-line to form a tent.

4 USE LARGE ROCKS, stakes or sticks to secure the corners of the tarpaulin, making sure to stretch the sides of your tent taut. Now you're ready to camp!

Building a raft

⚜ ⚜ ⚜

There are lots of stories of people surviving on rafts for weeks and months in the ocean after escaping from some deserted island, but that's not the type of raft we're going for here. Think Huckleberry Finn and Tom Sawyer – two boys who set off to find a little adventure along the Mississippi River.

You can build a raft big enough for you and a friend to float on in a weekend if you have all the right materials, including the right-sized logs. Recruit some friends to help out with finding the logs and fitting them all together. Bring all your logs close to the shore for the building process so that you can easily push the raft in the water when you've finished, rather than having to drag it down to the river first.

YOU WILL NEED

- A knife
- A saw
- An axe
- Rope
- About 20 logs, 2 m (6 ft) long and 15 cm (6 in) in diameter

---

STEPS

1 **FIND SOME FALLEN TREES.** Sawing or chopping down trees is going to take up too much time and zap all your exploration energy. You're looking for mid-size trees, roughly 15 cm (6 in) in diameter (a bit fatter than your leg) and about 2 m (6 ft) long. This is going to be a square raft 2 m (6 ft) long on each side.

2 MAKE A SQUARE WITH FOUR LOGS, using an axe to make notches at each end so that they fit together where they overlap.

3 LASH THE LOGS TOGETHER with rope at the corners using a clove hitch knot (see page 13) to secure them in place.

4 MAKE THE DECK OF THE RAFT by notching more logs to fit and laying them across the square. Lash them all in place. The deck logs shouldn't be too close to each other because you'll need room for the lashing.

④

5 LAY TWO MORE LOGS ACROSS THE TOPS of the ends of the deck logs and lash these into place to hold your deck together. Drag your raft to the water and launch!

⑤

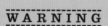

WARNING

Before launching your raft for distant ports of call, make sure you have a long pole you can use to steer the vessel by pushing off the bottom of the river.

Rowing a boat

⚜ ⚜

Before the invention of gas and steam engines, rowing boats were the most reliable way to navigate the rivers and lakes of the world that are too narrow to sail in. Because of that they were called the 'bicycles of the sea'. Rowing boats were the main form of river transport on the Thames in London, until they were mostly replaced by steam ferries in the 1850s. In nineteenth-century New York, 8-m (24-ft) long rowing boats hauled goods and sailors to and from the larger sailing vessels anchored off-shore. The same design of boat – called a 'Whitehall' boat – is still plying the waters there today.

Handling a rowing boat alone can be a daunting prospect, especially if you've never been in one or if you're dealing with river currents. Start out on quiet waters, and always bring along a First Mate. The two of you can also take fishing equipment to do some angling while you're out (see page 55).

YOU WILL NEED
- A rowing boat
- Oars

STEPS

1 SIT IN YOUR ROWING BOAT between the rowlocks, with your back facing the bow (front). There may be foot braces at your feet for extra leverage.

2 PUT THE OARS IN THE ROWLOCKS, take hold of the handles, and place your feet in the braces. Position the oars a little above the water, making sure that the oar blade is perpendicular to (forms a 'T' with) the surface.

3 NOW LEAN FORWARDS, slightly bending your knees, and extend your arms fully forward, so that the oar paddles are behind you.

4 DIP THE OAR BLADES INTO THE WATER and begin the stroke by slightly extending your legs.

5 USE YOUR BACK AND TORSO to carry the oars through the water, keeping your arms straight until you're sitting upright in the seat.

6 TO FINISH THE STROKE, bring your arms into your chest. The stroke should be a fluid movement that includes legs, back and arms.

WARNING

When rowing on rivers always row upstream to avoid rapids, and to make the trip back home easier.

Rowing isn't all fun and games – it's one of the most competitive sports in the world. In rowing races, however, they don't paddle in fishing dinghys or wooden tubs – they use sculls. These long, narrow boats cut right through the water like knives, and they come in different sizes, rowed by just one person or by as many as eight. With that many rowers everyone has to be in the same rhythm. To make that easier, there is a coxswain (or 'cox'), who sits in the back of the boat with a megaphone keeping everyone in time.

DID YOU KNOW? Nothing matches the fierce competitiveness of college rowing. In one style of boat race, called 'bumps', teams chase each other, trying to bump into the boat in front without getting bumped by the boat behind. Legend has it that, in 1876, one of the teams in a college race in Cambridge tied a sword to their boat, to try and sink an opposing team. Unfortunately, instead of poking a hole in the boat they ended up poking a hole in the cox! They were disqualified from racing ever again.

Ice skating

⚜⚜⚜

Learning how to skate can be hard (and so can the ice when you fall on it). But once you get the hang of it, you can set up goals, get some sticks and a puck and play hockey. If you really want to show off, you can even skate backwards!

Knowing how to skate starts with a snugly-fitting pair of ice skates. The general rule of thumb is to pick a skate about half a size smaller than your normal shoe size. Lace them up tight enough so that your ankles won't turn in, but not so tight that you cut off circulation to your feet.

Ever wondered why you can skate on a sheet of ice but not, say, on a concrete pavement? It's because of friction – the force that makes it hard to slide two surfaces against each other. Ice creates much less friction with other surfaces than concrete does – that's why when you walk on ice, you slip. And when you're on the ice using a thin blade of steel, rather than the bottom of your trainers, there's much less surface to rub against so you'll have even less friction. In fact, the thin edge of the skate creates enough pressure under your weight to melt the ice slightly, creating a thin layer of water that reduces the friction even further. So you see, skates are actually pretty clever inventions!

If there were no friction at all when you went ice skating, you'd simply step on the ice and keep going in that direction until you ran into the wall on the other side of the rink. There is a little friction, thankfully, which you can use to steer and change your speed. You can increase the friction between your skates and the ice (and therefore control your movements) by slightly leaning your blades over and digging an edge into the ice.

DID YOU KNOW? Before ice skating became a cold-weather leisure sport, early humans in modern-day Europe and Russia used animal bones strapped to their feet to make it easier to travel across frozen terrain. The Dutch are credited with inventing the metal blades we're all familiar with. The design was first seen in paintings from about 800 years ago and it hasn't changed much since.

YOU WILL NEED

● A frozen pond, river, lake or rink ● A pair of ice skates

STEPS – BEGINNER

1 TO STABILISE YOURSELF right away, use little side steps to work your way out onto the ice.

2 FIND YOUR BALANCE by keeping your feet slightly apart, with your knees bent and your arms extended in front of you. Bend slightly at the waist to keep your weight balanced front to back.

3 KEEPING THIS POSITION, point your toes slightly inwards until your feet come together. Then push your skates out until they glide out to shoulder width before pointing your toes inwards again to bring your skates back together.

4 REPEAT THESE MOTIONS and you should glide across the ice! This type of skating is called 'sculling'.

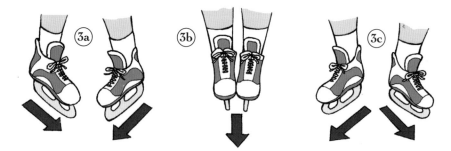

STEPS – INTERMEDIATE

1 ONCE YOU HAVE A FEEL FOR THE ICE, you can graduate to the more advanced left-right-left skating style. This will let you move faster and more smoothly, but be prepared to fall over a couple of times before you get the hang of it!

2 START BY BENDING YOUR KNEES and leaning on your left foot while pushing out and back on the ice with your right skate. You should start gliding forwards on your left skate.

3 NEXT, BEND YOUR KNEES and lean on your right foot and push out and back on the ice with your left skate.

4 REPEAT THE PROCESS and you should start to glide smoothly across the ice!

5 AS YOU GAIN IN CONFIDENCE, push a little harder with your back foot, to move yourself along a little faster.

6 STOP YOUR FORWARD MOMENTUM by holding one skate blade horizontally behind you.

WARNING

Falling on hard ice really hurts. If you think you're going to fall, bend your knees and try to slide down on your side rather than put your hands down.

STEPS – ADVANCED: BACKWARD SKATING

1 START WITH YOUR HEAD UP, knees bent and your back straight – the same position for the beginner steps, in fact.

2 THE IDEA IS TO 'SCULL' in the opposite direction, so point your heels in until your feet come together, then push them out to shoulder width. Getting someone to give you a gentle backward push can help you get started.

3 REPEAT THE MOTIONS as you did for sculling forwards: bring your heels together, then push your skates out, then bring them together again. Remember to keep an eye out behind you!

4 ALWAYS KEEP YOUR KNEES BENT and don't bend your waist forward or you could lose your balance.

5 WHEN YOU'RE FEELING TRULY CONFIDENT, you can try turning round as you skate, so you switch from going forwards to gliding backwards. This takes some practice, so be prepared for a few bruises before you get it right.

Predicting the weather

❧

Predicting the weather can be very useful if you're planning a day out in the open and want to avoid getting wet and frozen. And it's also a good way to impress your fellow travellers.

Cloud-reading

One way of doing this just requires you to know a little bit about the different types of clouds and how they act. There are four main types of clouds, and they are categorised depending on how high or low they float in the sky. The highest floating clouds – 5 km (16,500 ft) or higher – are in the cirrus family. **Cirrus clouds** are wispy and frozen and do not indicate bad weather.

Clouds floating in the middle range of the sky – 2 to 5 km (6,500 to 16,500 ft) high – are known as **alto clouds**. They look like large patchy sheets that cover big parts of the sky. Seeing these on a warm day usually indicates thunderstorms later.

The lowest-floating clouds include **stratus clouds**. They can reach as high as 2 km (6,500 ft), but some stratus clouds drop all the way to the surface of the planet and are known as fog. While stratus clouds don't necessarily forecast rain, some of the types of clouds in this family do. Nimbostratus clouds, for example, look grey and fluffy while covering the entire sky. You can expect rain in the next few hours if you see these.

The last type of cloud is the vertical cloud, which can reach from ground level up to several kilometres high. These are the **cumulus clouds**, known sometimes as thunderheads. They are white, puffy and massive, and as their name indicates they forecast thunder, lightning and heavy rain or hail. If you see these rolling in then watch out: a storm's brewing.

Cumulus clouds

Making a weather vane

Another good method of predicting the weather is to know which way the wind is blowing. A weather vane will help you gauge this accurately. Keep a log of the wind direction on rainy days and fine days and see if you can work out a pattern. If you know it always rains when the wind is in the south-west, you'll know what to expect the next time the wind blows from that direction.

YOU WILL NEED

- A broom handle
- A hammer and a 7.5-cm (3-in) nail
- A saw
- A 30-cm (12-in) length of wood, 5 x 10 cm (2 x 4 in)
- Pieces of plywood
- Wood glue

STEPS

1 CUT TWO PIECES OF PLYWOOD to make a triangle and a rectangle. Cut slits at each end of your length of wood, and glue the plywood shapes into the slits to make a wooden arrow.

2 HAMMER THE NAIL THROUGH the centre of your arrow. Turn the nail a few times until the hole loosens so the arrow can spin freely.

3 HAMMER THE REST OF THE NAIL into the broom handle. Plant it securely in the ground in a windy spot and use a compass to tell which direction the arrow is pointing – that's where the wind is coming from!

DID YOU KNOW? Clouds can be made up of more than just water. Volcanic eruptions throw up dust into the atmosphere that gets blown around and mixed up in clouds. Dust from the eruption of Krakatoa in 1883 caused blood-red sunsets all across the world!

Orienteering

— ✦✦ —

Every explorer from Magellan to Indiana Jones has had to know how to use a compass and read a map. In dire situations, many have even found their way without any tools, using shadows and the stars to guide them on their adventures. Whether you're setting out to conquer Mount Kilimanjaro or the hill behind your house, knowing how to get there – and get home – is a great skill to have.

Once you work out how to use a map and compass it'll be easy. Getting started, however, is a little complicated. After two or three outings you should have cracked it.

How to use a map and compass

You can probably already find your way with a road map, but it's a bit harder to use a map with no roads on it. These kinds of maps have a grid of lines over the top of them as if someone was dividing the map up into a bunch of squares. The up and down lines are north and south. The left to right lines are east and west. On some road-less maps you'll also notice lots of winding, curving lines that circle around certain places on the map. These tell you how the land drops off (for gorges or river beds) and how the land rises up (for hills and mountains). All maps have detailed legends or keys in a big box in one corner that will tell you what all the colours and lines mean. By referring to the key you can tell what kinds of trees, fields and rocks you can expect to find on your adventures.

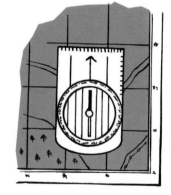

Next to a good map, a compass is a must on any long exploration. Invented in China over 1,000 years ago, this simple device uses the earth's magnetic field to tell you which way is north. Using a map and a compass together you should be able to find any buried treasure, secret hideout or lost city.

YOU WILL NEED

- A compass with a base plate
- A map

STEPS

1 PLACE YOUR MAP ON A TABLE and work out where you are (best to do this at base camp: maps will usually have paths, tracks and buildings marked on them to help).

2 LOCATE ON THE MAP A MOUNTAIN, field or lake that you want to explore.

3 NEXT, PUT YOUR COMPASS ON THE MAP and line up the sides of the compass base plate with an imaginary line going from your present location to your destination. This means the direction arrow at the top of the compass base plate should be pointing in the direction of your destination.

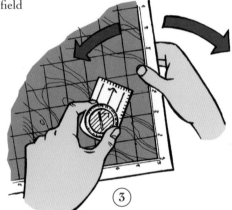

4 WITHOUT MOVING THE COMPASS BASE PLATE, rotate the central dial in the middle until its north arrow aligns itself with the compass's magnetic needle. This sets your bearing into the compass.

5 TO REACH YOUR DESTINATION, walk in the direction of the arrow on the base plate while ensuring that the magnetic needle is aligned with the north arrow on the compass.

6 AS YOU'RE WALKING, take note of your natural surroundings, like streams, buildings and areas of woodland. Then check to make sure they're on the map by referring to the key, so you know you're on the right track.

Finding north without a compass

❧

Lots of adventurers in history didn't have any instruments at all and they completed their missions. You can too! If you don't have a compass, you can find north using a few different methods.

Using a watch

YOU WILL NEED
- A watch

A watch can be made into a compass. Just hold it horizontal to the ground and point the hour hand directly at the sun. Then imagine a line running exactly in the middle between the hour hand and the 12 o'clock mark on your watch. That imaginary line points north and south – south being at the top of the line, which usually means you'll be facing south with north behind you.

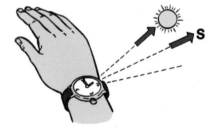

Northern hemisphere

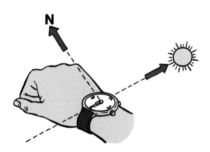

Southern hemisphere

If you're in the southern hemisphere point the watch's 12 o'clock mark in the direction of the sun and your north/south line will run between this and wherever the hour hand is. In this case, north is at the top of this line, meaning you'll probably be facing north with the southerly direction behind you.

If you have a digital watch, no problem! Draw out a watch with hands showing the right time on paper with a pencil. Then follow the same procedure using the clock you have drawn.

Using shadow sticks

Another method for finding directions is by reading shadows. It's pretty easy but you'll need at least 15 minutes to discover which way is north.

YOU WILL NEED
- A stick
- Two stones

STEPS

1 FIND A STRAIGHT, GOOD SIZE STICK, about 90 cm (3 ft) long, and plant it so it stands up straight in level ground where it can cast a clear shadow.

2 MARK THE TIP OF ITS SHADOW with one of your two stones. This will be your west mark.

3 WAIT AT LEAST 15 MINUTES, then go back and check the shadow's progress: it will have moved.

4 NOW MARK THE NEW SHADOW TIP with your other stone and you will have an east mark.

5 DRAW A LINE BETWEEN THE TWO MARKS for a west/east line. Draw another line exactly perpendicular to this one to form a north/south line.

6 BY PLACING YOUR LEFT FOOT at the west mark and your right foot at the east mark you will always be facing north. This rule applies anywhere in the world.

Navigating by the stars

The ancient Polynesians of the South Pacific may have been history's best navigators. They discovered and settled thousands of islands without any instruments at all – only the knowledge of the sky that was passed down from father to son through stories. Polynesian navigators, or *palus*, were required to train for a long time before they could navigate their own ships. One part of the training was memorising the colours of the sky and sea, the various clouds that would cluster over islands, and the stars. Here's how to follow their example.

YOU WILL NEED

- A clear night sky

STEPS – NORTHERN HEMISPHERE

1 FIND THE NORTH STAR, usually one of the brightest in the night sky, by first locating the Plough. Draw an imaginary line joining the two stars that form the Plough's front line, and continue this line out about five times its original length. You should arrive at the North Star.

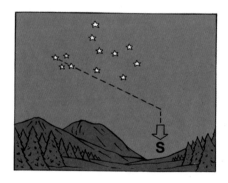

2 NOW JUST DRAW AN IMAGINARY LINE from the North Star down to earth. The Star sits directly over the North Pole, so that way is North.

STEPS – SOUTHERN HEMISPHERE

1 THERE IS NO NORTH STAR in the southern hemisphere. Instead, locate the constellation known as the Southern Cross, next to the constellation Centaurus.

2 ONCE YOU'VE PICKED OUT THE FOUR BRIGHT STARS that form the Cross, look to the two stars that make the longer of the two crossbeams. These will point your way.

3 EXTEND THIS CROSSBEAM out to five times its length and mark that imaginary point in the sky. A line drawn from that point down to earth will give you an approximate south reading.

Reading the night sky

Star-gazing has been a human pastime for as long as there have been humans. Eventually star-gazers turned into star-readers to try and make sense of it all. Constellations, or groups of stars, were a way to mark the seasons for the ancient Egyptians back in 2000 B.C. The Mesopotamians in 1000 B.C. began to map the night sky in more detail. Then a Greek man named Ptolemy, who lived in Roman Egypt, was the first to name what we in the Western world know as the constellations. Ptolemy is credited with naming the 12 signs of the Zodiac. The Chinese, meanwhile, were discovering and naming their own constellations.

Spotting planets

There are five planets that are visible to the naked eye – Mercury, Venus, Mars, Jupiter and Saturn. Astronomers in the past called these bright lights in the sky 'wandering stars', because they moved across the sky in different directions and at different speeds than the stars that make up the constellations. In fact 'planet' in Greek means 'wanderer'.

The planets are named after the Roman gods and were long ago thought to be actual living creatures. With the addition of the Sun and the Moon, the names of the planets (translated from Latin to Anglo-Saxon) gave us the seven days of the week. In China and Japan, the five planets are named after the five elements: Mercury is the water star, Venus is the metal star, Mars is the fire star, Jupiter is the wood star and Saturn is the earth star.

Mercury You can only see Mercury in the early morning or late afternoon, just before the sun comes up or just after it goes down. Look for Mercury in the direction of the sunset about 45 minutes after the sun dips beneath the horizon, or in the direction of sunrise about 45 minutes before the sun comes up. The best times for viewing in the northern hemisphere are March and April (during sunset) and September and October (during sunrise). The opposite is true if you're planet-spotting in the southern hemisphere, where the best times to spot Mercury are sunrise in March and April, and sunset in September and October.

Venus Venus is always the third brightest object in the sky after the Sun and Moon and is known alternately as the Morning or Evening Star. Venus can also be seen by looking in the direction of the setting or rising sun, and it is visible for much longer periods of time than Mercury.

Mars Mars is visible all night and is brightest every two years, when its orbit is closest to the Earth's and it is in opposition to our planet (in other words, the Earth is between it and the Sun). The planet follows the same path as the sun across the night sky and is most visible looking east in the early morning. You can recognise it by its orange-red colour.

Jupiter Even though it's much further away, Jupiter is the next brightest object in the sky after Venus because it's so large – 1,300 times the volume of the Earth! Like Venus it is best seen during twilight hours. Those with a telescope might be able to see Jupiter's large red spot, which is actually a colossal storm twice the size of Earth.

Saturn Because Saturn is so far away (10 times further away from the Sun than Earth), it's hard to see unless you know where to look. It's at its brightest when its rings are fully facing the Earth, but that last happened in 2002 and won't happen again until 2017. For now, look for a pale yellow star low in the western sky at around dusk.

Uranus, **Neptune** and **Pluto** The three outermost planets in the Solar System are hard to see without a telescope. Pluto is now actually classified as a dwarf planet, much smaller than the others in the Solar System, and impossible to see with the naked eye.

Constellations

There are actually 88 different constellations mapped out all across the sky from Pole to Pole, east and west. The constellations you can see are different in the northern and southern hemispheres, because the curve of the Earth hides some stars from us. You can look up star charts on the Internet or your local library, which will tell you exactly where to look for constellations in different places and at different times of year. They can also tell you when to look for exciting events like meteor showers, or a lunar eclipse! It's best to do your star-spotting away from cities, though, since light pollution from street lights in urban areas makes it hard to see faint objects in the skies.

The Zodiac and astrology

The constellations of the Zodiac can be found roughly along the path that the Sun takes across the sky, like a band around the Earth. They have been identified and studied by human civilizations for thousands of years. They are called: **Aries** (the ram), **Taurus** (the bull), **Gemini** (the twins), **Cancer** (the crab), **Leo** (the lion), **Virgo** (the virgin), **Libra** (the scales), **Scorpio** (the scorpion), **Sagittarius** (the archer), **Capricorn** (the goat), **Aquarius** (the water-bearer) and **Pisces** (the fish).

Each one has its own meanings and symbol, which you can see in the chart below. They are the basis for astrology, a system that many people believe can predict the future by the movements of the stars. Each symbol is most visible at a particular time of year, and people born during that time are said to have characteristics of that symbol. Find your birthday on the list below to see what star sign you are.

You can find the predictions of your future based on the Zodiac (called your 'horoscope') in many newspapers. Look up your star-sign and see what the future holds. It's up to you to decide how accurate the predictions really are.

Capricorn: 23 December–20 January
Aquarius: 21 January–19 February
Pisces: 19 February–20 March
Aries: 21 March–20 April
Taurus: 21 April–21 May
Gemini: 22 May–21 June
Cancer: 22 June–23 July
Leo: 24 July–23 August
Virgo: 24 August–23 September
Libra: 24 September–23 October
Scorpio: 24 October–22 November
Sagittarius: 23 November–22 December

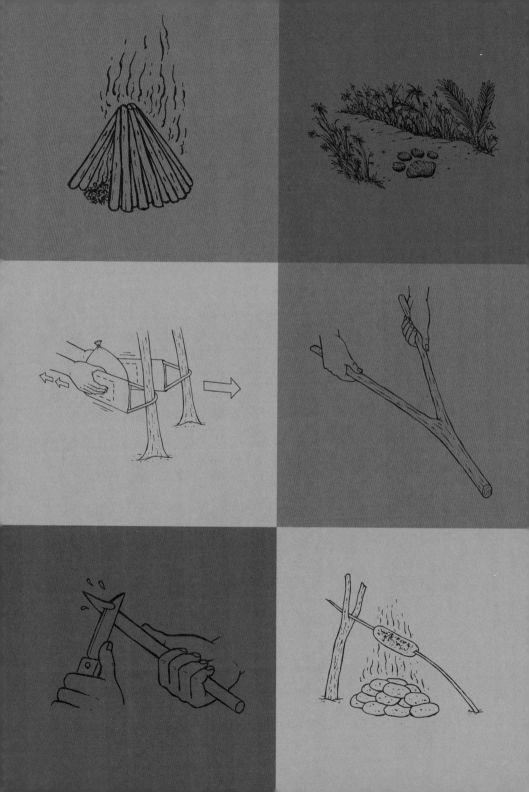

Chapter Two

Hunting

ANY HEROIC ADVENTURER IS USUALLY SEEKING
something. They may have a lot of excitement
along the way, but there's usually a buried
treasure, hidden secret or lost empire that got
them out into the world in the first place.

✦

For those of us who don't know of any local pirate
booty or lost cities to uncover, there's always the
world's natural treasures to hunt for. Animals,
shells and exploring the contents of a nearby
stream can be as fun and mysterious as any
expedition to the North Pole (and a lot warmer).

✦

So pack up your bow and arrow, brush up on your
fire-building and fishing skills, and get ready for a
few days of nature hunting. You never know what
you might discover.

Making a bow and arrow

Bows and arrows have been around for tens of thousands of years, and were the most efficient long-range weapon in existence until the invention of the rifle. A real archer's bow is the result of many hours of work, but you can construct a short-term bow for target practice fairly easily. When it loses its spring or breaks, you can replace it by making another.

YOU WILL NEED

- A penknife
- Straight lengths of wood 60 cm (2 ft) long, for arrow shafts
- A straight length of strong, springy wood 1.2 m (4 ft) long,

and no more than 2 cm (¾ in) thick, for the bow
- 90 cm (3 ft) of cord, shoelace or any other tough string
- Feathers

To make the arrows

1 TAKE YOUR ARROW SHAFT and make it as straight as possible, by cutting off twigs or nubs and stripping away the bark. Sharpen one end to a point with your knife.

2 CUT A NOTCH IN THE OTHER END, about 0.5 cm (¼ in) deep, so that you can fit the arrow on the bowstring.

3 CUT A FEATHER IN HALF, and cut each half into 1 cm (½ in) lengths. Tie three of these to the notched end of your arrow to help it fly straight.

How to make the bow

1 CHECK THAT THE WOOD is free of knots or limbs. Scrape it down so that the wood is smooth, and trim it to be a little thinner at the ends. Take note of the natural curve of the wood – scrape from the side that will face you when you use the bow, or it will break the first time you pull it.

2 CUT NOTCHES ON EACH SIDE at the head and foot of the bow, 5 cm (2 in) from each end. Cut them just deep enough to hold the bowstring so it doesn't slip.

3 ATTACH THE BOWSTRING to one notched end with a good all-around knot like the clove hitch (see page 13). Tie a bowline (see page 12) in the other end of the string to make a small loop.

4 NOW COMES THE TRICKY PART. Brace the tied end of the bow against your foot, and hold the other end of the stick and the string loop in each hand. Pull the bow down, then slip your bowline loop over the end and into the notches.

How to shoot an arrow

1 TAKE YOUR ARROW and place in the bow, with the end of the arrow notched onto the bowstring.

2 HOLD THE BOW up in front of you and look down the length of the arrow at your target.

3 DRAW THE BOWSTRING BACK to your ear, keeping the arrow steady along the bow with your thumb.

4 RELEASE THE BOWSTRING and the arrow, and watch the arrow sail off into the air.

WARNING

A bow and arrow is a lethal weapon. Never point it at a person, and always set up your target away from other people.

Making a catapult

Catapults were invented in China and Greece around the fourth century B.C. – small ones for hunting and larger ones for hurling rocks at the enemy in wartime. Although catapults have made brief appearances in war since the Middle Ages – once during World War I when French troops used them to launch hand grenades – they mostly died out with the invention of cannons.

In Medieval times, catapults were used to bombard castles, to bring down the walls and attack people inside. There are records of catapults being used to launch rocks, fireballs, diseased animals (to spread plague among the enemy), and even hives full of angry bees!

On a hot summer day, you can use the same technology to cool off – or cool off your friends – with a water balloon catapult.

YOU WILL NEED
- 3 m (10 ft) of rubber tubing
- An old pair of jeans
- A needle and fishing line
- Water-filled balloons

STEPS

1 TIE THE ENDS OF THE RUBBER TUBING together to make a giant loop. (Remember the reef knot from page 12.)

2 CUT OFF A 25-CM (10-INCH) LONG SECTION of leg from an old pair of jeans. This will be the launch pad for your balloons.

3 SLIDE ONE LEG of the jeans over the rubber tubing loop, and centre it on the tubing so that an equal loop of rubber sticks out on each side.

4 THREAD A NEEDLE WITH FISHING LINE. Then sew a line in the jeans leg right next to where the tubing goes through the trouser leg. This keeps the jeans leg from moving up or down the tubing.

LAUNCHING A WATER BALLOON

1 HAVE TWO FRIENDS hold the ends of the rubber tubing, or tie both ends of the tubing to two trees or posts.

2 FILL A BALLOON halfway up with water and tie it off. In fact, fill up a few so you've got a store of ammo handy.

3 PLACE THE BALLOON on the jeans-leg launch pad. Hold it in place and get ready to fire.

4 USING TWO HANDS, grab the leg where the tubing runs through it and pull back as far as you want. (To ensure the balloon doesn't roll out, you'll have to pull back and down.)

5 LET GO WITH BOTH HANDS and watch the balloon fly!

6 TRY LAUNCHING AT DIFFERENT angles up and down to achieve maximum range and accuracy. You could mount one in your treehouse and use it to bombard would-be invaders!

Making a slingshot

You can make a miniature, hand-held slingshot after the same design by finding a sturdy forked twig, and winding elastic around the forks over and over in a figure eight. Sew a patch of leather, or another piece of old jeans, in a circle round the middle of the figure-of-eight to launch your ammunition. You can use this contraption to fire small pebbles.

In the olden days, slingshots like this were sometimes used to hunt small animals and birds, but because pebbles are all different shapes and sizes, slingshots aren't very accurate. You can try knocking cans or bottles off a wall for some fun target practice. Just be careful there's nobody in the way or walking behind, because a pebble to the head can be very painful.

Building a hideout

You can use a hideout to watch for animals and birds. Or you can keep it as base camp for your adventures, and as a place to store your adventuring supplies. Even just building and playing inside one can be great fun.

A hideout can be built from a cardboard box, inside a thick patch of bushes, or claimed in a hollow tree in the woods, or set up in the loft. Wherever you decide to build, seclusion is the key to a good hideout. It should be somewhere less travelled and not easily seen by the casual passerby. You could build one behind the shrubbery beside your house, in a wood thicket, or in the attic.

All manner of materials can be used to construct a hideout, depending on where you want to build it. If you're outdoors and want to be protected from the elements, try stringing up a tarpaulin between two trees (see page 26). If you don't expect to see much rain, cardboard could be your material of choice. A collection of large boxes can be linked together with tape, and you can cut out doors and windows. Use your imagination – anything that can be used to create a sense of private space will do.

After constructing your shelter, you may want to install some basic furniture – old cable spools make great tables. Rocks or wooden boxes can be chairs. A coldbox may also come in handy – it can double as a chair and you can store provisions in it. When you're away from your hideout, a few well-placed limbs from a nearby tree or bush will cover up your structure nicely.

Hideouts make great base camps for your adventures, and a good place to store your adventuring equipment. They're also a good way to conceal yourself if you're watching for birds or animals. Many species will be scared off by the sight of a human being, so making a hideout amongst the natural vegetation will increase your chances of seeing something.

Choose somewhere you know the animal or bird you're waiting to see likes to go. Use a large box, or rig up a small tent (see page 26), and cover it with leaves and branches of the local vegetation. Then climb inside and wait quietly to see what comes along.

Birdwatching

✦

Sometimes sneaking up on an animal just to see it in its natural surroundings is as satisfying as catching one. It's also a lot easier, especially when it comes to birds. Birds are fascinating creatures: from tiny hummingbirds to huge eagles, they come in every colour of the rainbow and are found on every continent.

Seeing birds in detail can be a challenge, both because they're hard to get close to and because they're often well camouflaged, especially on the ground. And if you don't know what you're looking for many of them may look the same. Here's a few tips on how to spot and identify them.

YOU WILL NEED
- A pair of good binoculars
- A guide to birds in your region
- A pad and pencil

STEPS

1 PACK YOUR EQUIPMENT and set off. Head for somewhere near to water, or to a food source like trees with fruit or berries, where birds naturally congregate.

2 EITHER SET UP A HIDEOUT (SEE PAGE 50), or find somewhere sheltered, so you can sit comfortably and wait quietly for the birds to arrive.

3 WHEN YOU SPOT AN INTERESTING BIRD, train the binoculars on it to get a magnified view. Make notes about its size, the shape of its beak, any markings around the head and chest, and the shape of its tail feathers.

4 LIKE ALL ANIMALS, different birds are found in different regions. Use a guide to the birds in your region to identify what you've seen from your notes. Serious birdwatchers keep a log of exactly what they've seen and where, so if they want to see a particular bird again, they know where to go.

Tracking

✦

Tracking animals and birds requires a powerful sense of awareness and observation. There are footprints to recognise, but that's the easy part. Skilled trackers also know how to find and follow all kinds of signs, symbols and clues, such as fur or feathers, broken sticks and leaves and animal scents and dung.

Animal prints

If you discover some tracks in snow, mud or sand, you'll want to know what kind of animal you're up against. Bears and large cats spell danger not adventure, so don't set up camp anywhere you spot their tracks. Deer, rabbits, foxes and other small furry creatures are mostly harmless, and it can be good fun to track them back to their lair.

Wild dogs like foxes and wolves always have diamond-shaped paws that are longer than they are wide. Plus, they have four toes tipped by claw marks. Big cats, on the other hand have retractable claws that won't show up in the mud (they also have four toes). Another characteristic of the big cats, like lions or jaguars, is that their toe marks are more circular than those of dogs. Bear prints have five toes with claw marks. They're also going to be significantly bigger than those of a fox or wildcat. Look across the page for some sample tracks.

How to track

Animals often use the same routes over and over, even if their territory covers hundreds of square miles. This makes things easier for the tracker – if you spot a well-used path, you can follow it to pick up the animal's trail. Of course, that all changes if the animal knows you're there – then they'll likely change course or hide. That's why tracking takes plenty of practice and patience.

Scientists have been tracking the movements of birds and animals for centuries, and even they've had to learn on the job. In the old days, scientists would tie string markers to the legs of migrating birds to see if they would return to the same spot a year later (they often did.) Now scientists attach radio tags to all kinds of animals – from elephants and big cats to whales and dolphins – to track their movements all over the world by satellite.

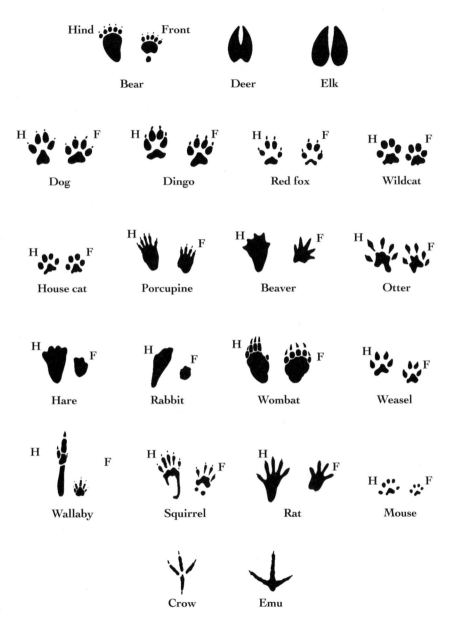

Hind Front

Bear Deer Elk

H F
Dog

H F
Dingo

H F
Red fox

H F
Wildcat

H F
House cat

H F
Porcupine

H F
Beaver

H F
Otter

H F
Hare

H F
Rabbit

H F
Wombat

H F
Weasel

H F
Wallaby

H F
Squirrel

H F
Rat

H F
Mouse

Crow Emu

Since most of us don't have access to electronic tags or satellites, we'll have to track like the primitive hunters in the old days. To follow an animal's trail, walk next to its prints, keeping the tracks between you and the sun so your shadow doesn't obscure them. Sometimes tracks can become faint, especially in drier weather, so try looking ahead of you to spot additional signs like broken foliage, flattened grass or dung. Stay as quiet as you can: talk in a whisper and avoid walking on dry twigs or leaves. Lastly, try to think like an animal. If you lose the trail in a natural boundary like a river or gorge, look for the easiest natural way forward – ask yourself what the animal would have done and follow your instincts until you catch up with the tracks again.

Often the tracks will stop at a burrow or watering place – if you wait there quietly (especially at dusk) there's a good chance you'll see your animal when it wakes up or decides it wants a drink. If you're lucky, and move quietly enough while you're tracking, you might catch up with whatever you're following, especially if it's stopping to graze or drink along the way. Then you can take a photo or just admire the creature – the best moment for any tracker.

DID YOU KNOW? Dinosaur footprints from millions of years ago have been preserved as fossils. These fossils, called 'ichnites', tell us about the way different dinosaurs moved around.

Fishing

Because it's loaded with protein and vitamins, fish is an ideal food when out on a big adventure. But even if you don't plan to eat what you catch, fishing is fun. Land one just to observe the underwater creature and then return him to his watery life.

How to make a fishing rod

It's not the only way to catch a fish, but a fishing rod is the easiest. With a few supplies and a long straight stick, you can make a good one in less than an hour.

YOU WILL NEED
- A 3-m (10-ft) long stick or bamboo cane
- A fishing line
- A fishing hook and float (old corks make good floats)

STEPS

1 FIRST, YOU NEED TO FIND THE RIGHT KIND OF STICK. Bamboo works well because it can bend just enough without breaking if you catch a big one. Otherwise, a trimmed tree branch will do fine.

2 CUT A LENGTH OF LINE about the same length as your pole. Fishing line is strong and light, but very thin so fish can't see it in the water.

3 TIE THE FISHING LINE around the narrow end of your stick (the thicker end is your handle).

4 TIE THE LINE ROUND YOUR FLOAT about 30 cm (1 ft) from the end. Tie the hook to the very end of your line, and you're ready for some bait.

Bait

If you can find a worm, use that to bait your hook. Fish love worms. If you can't find one, there are lots of other things a fish will gladly bite. Pay attention to your surroundings. More often than not fish dine on the insects and vegetation that is locally available. Your chances of catching a fish will be better if you tempt them with something familiar.

POTENTIAL BAIT:
- Worm
- Grasshopper
- Fly
- Berry
- Bit of bread
- Cheese
- Pasta

How to Bait a Hook

You don't have to use professional hooks to catch a fish. Bent nails, pins, pieces of wire and even sharp thorns work just as well.

1. TO HOOK A WORM, thread the hook through the head and run the hook through the body until the end is in the worm's tail.

2. IF YOUR WORMS AREN'T BIG ENOUGH to thread over the hook in this manner, you can use several worms – just be sure to fully cover the hook.

3. FOR INSECTS, use a segment of thin metal wire and wrap the bait around the hook. Do not damage the insect's body.

4. TO BAIT SMALL LIVE FISH or minnows, slide the hook in through the lower and upper lip or along the back (but avoid the spine). Both these techniques allow the fish to stay alive and swim as it normally would, which is appealing for the larger fish you're trying to catch.

Lures

If you can't find a worm, the grasshoppers keep eluding capture, and you've eaten all the other potential bait, use a lure. Fish will often bite something that just *looks* like their normal food.

POTENTIAL LURES

- Feather
- Bottle cap
- Button
- Tin foil

Simply attach a lure to your hook right above its end, in the hope that the fish will swallow the whole thing.

Angling

Knowing where and how to fish is the next step on this adventure. With a home-made rod and simple bait, you're going to be limited to just dropping your line in the water. Even so, you can take a strategic approach to landing some swimmers. Here are a few pointers:

1 LOOK FOR STUMPS, large rocks and vegetation – these are good places to drop your line. Fish are hunters too, so they're going to be hiding in these nooks and crannies to surprise their prey.

2 WHEN FISHING IN THE MORNING, especially in cooler weather, fish near the water's surface by tying your float closer to the hook.

3 IN HOTTER WEATHER, or later in the day, fish in deeper waters and try and get your line down as far as possible by tying your float closer to the rod.

4 MOVE THE BAIT SLOWLY through the water, as though it's alive and swimming. Fish prefer live prey.

5 WHEN YOU SEE YOUR FLOAT DIP BELOW THE SURFACE, that means you've got a bite! Pull up on the rod so the hook catches, and little by little pull your prey to shore. Don't pull so hard that the line breaks, or all your hard work will be for nothing.

Building a fire

⚜⚜

When out on a fishing adventure, the hope is you'll catch what you're looking for and then cook it. And if the fish aren't biting, you'll still need to take a break and warm up by the campfire. Building a fire takes real skill and care. Where you locate the fire is as important as how you build it.

Fires should be in areas that are relatively out of the wind and well away from low-hanging limbs and dry grasses. Before you get started, clear a circle about 2 m (6 ft) in diameter of any undergrowth, and scrape it down until you reach bare soil. Then dig a shallow fire pit at the centre of the circle and surround it with rocks. This makes sure you only burn what you mean to – the basic rule of fire safety.

YOU WILL NEED ⚠
- A cricket-ball-sized bundle of tinder, like dried grass, wood shavings or even bits of fur
- Pencil-sized twigs and sticks
- Medium-sized sticks
- Four large logs
- Matches

STEPS

1 PUT YOUR BUNDLE OF TINDER at the centre of your fire pit. Use pencil-sized pieces of kindling to make a small teepee over the tinder bed.

2 BUILD THE TEEPEE OUT using gradually larger and larger pieces of wood. Don't use pieces of wood that are fatter than your wrist or you'll risk the teepee collapsing. Finish off with four larger logs in a square.

3 ONCE THE TEEPEE is finished, light the tinder at its centre.

Lighting a fire without matches

❧ ❧ ❧

Modern matches were invented in England in 1827 by a man named John Walker. Before that, anyone who wanted to start a fire had to do it without matches, either by striking sparks from flint or rubbing two sticks together. The Native Americans devised a technique called the bow and drill in which they used a bow, similar to the bows they used with arrows only much smaller, and a long piece of wood to 'drill' into another piece of wood called the hearth. The friction between the drill and hearth creates enough heat to ignite fur, dried grass and leaves and other tinder. It's not easy but it will work as long as you're willing to find the right materials and put some energy into the drilling. This technique works best when the drill and the hearth are dry and made of the same type of wood.

YOU WILL NEED

- A teepee of tinder and kindling
- A straight stick of hardwood for the drill
- A flat piece of dry hardwood for the hearth
- A 30-cm (1-ft) long stick of flexible wood for the bow
- A cord, shoelace or any other length of tough string
- A hand-sized piece of hardwood to use as the socket (this is what you'll hold to press down on the drill when you're turning it)
- A knife
- A strong piece of bark
- Tinder

STEPS

1 BEFORE STARTING, make sure you're positioned close to your teepee of tinder and kindling. Once you get an ember you'll need to transfer it quickly to the fire.

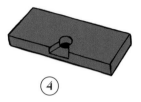

2 START MAKING YOUR BOW and drill by whittling one end of the drill into a point. Round off the other end.

3 CUT A SMALL HOLE halfway along the hearth about 2.5 cm (1 in) from an edge. The hole should be big enough to allow the rounded end of the drill to fit inside it.

4 NEXT CUT A TRIANGULAR NOTCH in the hearth from the hole to the nearest edge. This will serve as a channel for ashes and embers to spill out onto your tinder.

5 YOU'RE GOING TO USE THE SOCKET to press down firmly on the drill. To stop it from slipping, cut a small hole in the socket so that the rounded end of the drill will fit there snugly.

6 TIE THE CORD OR SHOELACE TO THE BOW. It's helpful to find a bow stick that's already bent but a freshly-cut stick should bend as you tie on the cord.

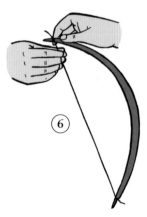

7 **PLACE THE HEARTH ON THE GROUND** so that the notched side is in contact with a small but strong piece of bark (this is where you will collect the embers).

8 **PLACE THE POINTED END OF THE DRILL** in the hole on the hearth. Loop the bow cord over the drill and turn the bow over so that the cord wraps once round the drill. Push down firmly on top of the drill with the socket.

9 **MAKE SAWING MOTIONS** with the bow to work the drill back and forth in a not-too-fast, not-too-slow, steady rhythm. Make sure the drill stays in contact with the hearth. This gets tiring so you may want Dad or a friend to take a turn.

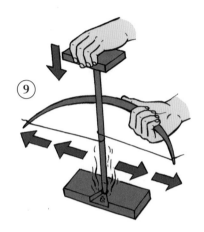

10 **EVENTUALLY THE FRICTION** will cause smoke to form and dark brown smoking powder should start rolling down the notch and onto the bark. When smoke appears, increase speed and pressure on the drill.

11 **ONCE THE NOTCH IS FILLED** with smoking powder and the powder is smoking on its own, gently move the hearth away from the bark and smoking powder. Place the smoking powder onto a small but tight ball of tinder and blow on it until it turns into a glowing red ember. The tinder should also begin to catch fire.

12 **QUICKLY TAKE THE SMOLDERING BALL** of tinder to the teepee of tinder and kindling and place it gently on the tinder platform. Blow on it more if need be until the kindling catches.

Campfire cooking

❧

For today's adventurer, it's always satisfying to make a fire and cook a meal at the end of a day's exploring. The best way to cook on a campfire is to use a long, sturdy, pointed stick. Almost anything can be skewered and held over the flame to cook. The other essential is tin foil. Wrap up some grub and set it on some hot coals to cook. Then again, it never hurts to have a frying pan handy. And don't forget the salt and pepper.

DID YOU KNOW? On large expeditions, adventurers always bring along a cook to keep the camp fed. In the American Wild West, during cattle drives from Texas to Chicago, the cowboys brought along mobile kitchens. Food back then was known as 'chuck' so the carts that carried the chuck were called 'chuck wagons'. Some say that the first chuck wagon was invented by legendary cattleman Charles Goodnight in 1866, who loaded a hinged box onto the back of an army wagon and filled it with kitchen supplies.

In general the best time to cook on an open fire is when the coals are glowing hot and bright – cooking directly on flames tends to leave your dinner black on the outside and raw in the middle.

Fish

YOU WILL NEED

- A freshly caught fish
- A frying pan
- A fork
- A plate
- Flour
- Salt and pepper
- Cooking oil or butter

STEPS

1 **PUT COOKING OIL OR BUTTER** in a frying pan and set it on a patch of good hot coals to heat.

2 **CUT YOUR FISH OPEN** and take out the insides. Cut off the head and tail, and cut the meat lengthwise into fillets.

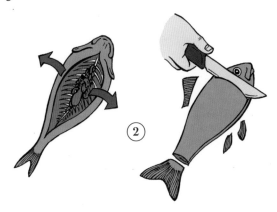

3 **MIX FLOUR,** salt and pepper on your plate. Pat each side of the fillets in the flour, then shake off the excess.

4 **TEST TO SEE IF THE OIL IS HOT** by putting a drop of water in it. If it crackles and pops it's ready.

5 **GENTLY PLACE** the fillets in the pan and cook them until each side is golden brown.

6 **USE A FORK TO TURN** the fillets over halfway through. The fish is cooked when the flesh flakes easily with a fork.

7 **WHEN THE FISH IS COOKED,** scoop the fillets out of the pan and eat them straight away with bread or potatoes (see page 64).

Potatoes

Almost anything can be added to this potato dish, from cheese to herbs to bacon and fish. Use your imagination and make something you'll enjoy.

YOU WILL NEED

- Potatoes
- Butter
- Salt and pepper
- Tin foil
- A knife
- A hot campfire

STEPS

1 CUT THE POTATOES either into long French-fry like strips or into 0.5-cm (¼-in) thick rounds.

2 PUT THE BUTTER, potatoes, salt and pepper into a piece of tin foil and seal it shut. Place the foil packet on the ground right next to some hot coals.

3 COOK THE POTATOES for about an hour. Keep turning the foil packet every now and again so that the potatoes cook on all sides and don't burn.

S'mores

These popular American desserts are a welcome treat at the end – or the beginning – of a good hunt.

YOU WILL NEED

- Marshmallows
- Chocolate
- Wheatmeal biscuits
- A long sharp stick
- A hot fire

STEPS

1 GET OUT TWO WHEATMEAL BISCUITS and break off a square of chocolate about the same size. Place the chocolate square on one biscuit, keeping the other biscuit handy.

2 PUSH A MARSHMALLOW onto the sharp end of a long stick. Hold it just above the flames of the campfire until its outer surface starts to brown, char or even catch fire.

3 ONCE THE MARSHMALLOW IS HOT AND GOOEY, place it on top of the chocolate-covered biscuit. Use the second biscuit to pinch the marshmallow off the stick.

4 WAIT BRIEFLY until the hot marshmallow begins to melt the chocolate into a wonderfully gooey mess before eating.

Sausages

One of the best foods to take along on any expedition is a stick of peperoni or dried salami. Wrap it in greaseproof paper, seal it up in an airtight bag, and it'll last several days on the trail. Plus it doesn't require cooking.

The kind of sausages that do require cooking can be a tasty meal too. Simply run a sharp stick through the length of each sausage and cook them over hot coals until the outsides are crisp and browned. They can either be eaten by themselves or placed in a bun to make a sausage sandwich. Add mustard for a meal with more flavour.

WARNING

Raw fish and meat can make you ill if they're not properly cooked. Make sure all your food is good and hot all the way through before you take a bite.

Beachcombing

❖

Hunting along the surf and dunes of a beach for flotsam and jetsam – the lost, discarded treasures that wash up on shore – can provide hours of adventure, as well as a few prizes you can take back to the hideout or hang around your neck for good luck.

YOU WILL NEED
- A local tide table
- A bag for your collection
- A small garden rake or shovel

STEPS

1 CHECK THE LOCAL TIDE TABLE. The best time to go is a little bit before low tide, since the sea drops its treasures as the tide goes out.

2 TO INCREASE YOUR CHANCES of finding good stuff, check peninsulas and sand bars (which will be visible when the tide is out).

3 GO IN WINTER if possible since you're more likely to find a beach that isn't crowded. The days after big storms are also good times to hunt.

4 USE A SMALL RAKE or shovel to dig out possible shells and other treasures when you see the tips of them sticking up.

The combination of salt water and sand makes even ordinary things look strange and exciting. Pieces of wood can be bleached to look like dinosaur bones, and even bits of old glass can look like jewels. There are also lots of animal treasures along the beach: seashells, crab skeletons, shark's egg-cases. Collect the interesting things that you find and use a library or the Internet to identify them.

Some trees, like coconut palms, have seeds or fruit designed to float many miles and grow wherever they wash up. This is called 'sea dispersal', and explains why coconut palms grow on so many ocean shores across the globe. Coconuts have even been recorded washing up on beaches in Newfoundland and England!

Insect-hunting

❦

Finding insects isn't hard – there are over one million species of insect in the world, from beetles, bees and ants to grasshoppers, butterflies and praying mantises. And that's not even counting other creepy-crawlies like spiders and centipedes. So if you're not the squeamish type, find a jar and go hunting.

All kinds of fascinating creatures await – but be warned, some of them are pretty ugly. One of the world's largest insects is the giant weta, from New Zealand. They can be up to 20 cm (8 in) long and weigh up to 70 g (2.5 oz) – that's bigger than a sparrow!

YOU WILL NEED

- A glass jar with a lid
- A piece of cardboard
- A magnifying glass
- A pencil and notebook

STEPS

1 THE BEST TIME TO LOOK FOR INSECTS is late spring to early autumn – most species hibernate in winter. Look under rocks and in damp, shady areas.

2 ONCE YOU FIND AN INSECT you like, gently pick it up (using the cardboard if you don't want to touch it), drop it in the jar and put the lid on.

3 SKETCH THE INSECT and take notes. Compare your notes later with an encyclopedia or Internet guide to find out what you've caught.

4 YOU SHOULD LET YOUR INSECTS GO after you've had a chance to study them. Insects need the great outdoors to survive.

WARNING

Don't forget that some insects, like ants, wasps, bees and scorpions, can give nasty bites or stings.

Divining

If you ever get stuck on an extended adventure in the desert, or stranded on a Pacific island with no way back home, you'll need water. While we can go for a week or more without food, the body won't make it for more than three days without a drink. You can find water using a mysterious old technique called 'divining', or you can look where it occurs naturally.

For hundreds of years there have been people who claimed they could find water by walking in an open field and holding a Y-shaped stick above the ground until it pointed downwards. There is no scientific explanation behind the practice, but that doesn't seem to stop people from actually finding water by divining. That might be why it's also known as 'water witching'. Somehow diviners can sense energy fluctuations in the earth, and they've been known to find metal deposits and oil as well as water.

DID YOU KNOW? Water covers over 70 per cent of the Earth's surface and is also plentiful in space. Scientists think there are massive ice deposits on some of the moons of Jupiter and Saturn, and entire asteroids made of ice orbiting the Sun between Mars and Jupiter. One way of making Mars habitable by humans might be to crash ice-asteroids into the planet's surface to thicken the atmosphere and make it more like ours.

YOU WILL NEED
- A Y-shaped stick or bent coat-hanger
- A shovel
- Patience

STEPS

1 HOLD THE STICK out in front of you with two hands, one on each branch of the 'Y'. Make sure the stick is parallel to the ground. Walk slowly and clear your mind.

2 WHEN YOU BEGIN TO FEEL the stick pull downwards, you've reached a spot where underground water might be. Get digging and see what you find . . .

Natural signs of fresh water

If you aren't having any luck with a Y-shaped stick, look for natural signs of fresh water. When you do find water make sure you sterilise it thoroughly before you drink it, by boiling it for at least five minutes. Otherwise you'll get sick, and end up just as badly off – if not worse – than you were before.

1 ONE THING TO REMEMBER is that downhill leads to water. Check the bottoms of gorges or hollows between hills.

2 AREAS WITH DENSE vegetation are good places to look for water too. Or you can look for animal tracks – they often lead to water.

3 BAMBOO COLLECTS WATER. If you find a patch of it, bend the top of one stalk over into a container for the water to drain out

4 CACTI ARE ALSO GOOD SOURCES OF WATER. Just cut off the top to access the pulp and squeeze the water out of it into a container.

5 ICE AND SNOW in general are not good to eat because you'll lower your body temperature, and if it's dirty it can cause diarrhoea. Melt and sterilise it first.

6 IF YOU RUN ACROSS A DRIED RIVER BED, dig down a few feet in the sand until it begins to get wet. Dig deeper and water will begin to seep into your hole.

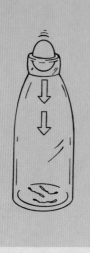

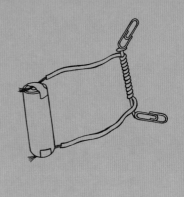

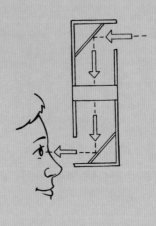

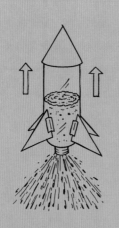

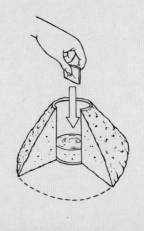

Chapter Three

Experimenting

IF YOU HAVE A CURIOUS MIND, ADVENTURE AND EXPLORATION
don't have to take place outdoors. Mad science
experiments can bring all the excitement you
could want.

✦

Try making your own paper and then sending secret
messages on it using invisible ink. Or you can create
your own special effects by building a volcano and
making it erupt, or by creating disgusting
green slime.

✦

Make a ping-pong ball float in the air or force a boiled
egg through the neck of a bottle – twice – and you're
definitely going to impress your friends.

Launching a bottle rocket

✦✦✦

The pinnacle of adventurous experimentation has got to be launching a rocket into the air. Maybe that's because, as grounded humans, we're fascinated with flight, and any chance we have to make something that can fly gives us a real thrill.

One of the easiest rockets to make is known as a water or bottle rocket. By pressurising air inside a plastic bottle that has a little water in it, you can send the device flying surprisingly high into the air. The air pushes the water out of the bottle with enough force to launch it. The rocket takes about an hour to make.

DID YOU KNOW? Rockets have been in use since long before aeroplanes. One of the first widely used rockets was invented by British Colonel William Congreve in 1801. Explosives attached to the ends of Congreve rockets were launched against Napoleon's armies in 1806. The world record height for a plastic bottle rocket is 582 m (1,909 ft), set in New York state by the US Water Rockets team, which launched at a speed of well over 160 kmph (100 mph)!

YOU WILL NEED

- A large plastic bottle
- A rubber stopper with a small hole in its centre, which can fit snugly in the mouth of the bottle
- A 30-cm (1-ft) long straw 6 mm (¼ in) in diameter
- Paint
- Clear plastic packing tape
- Scissors
- Sturdy cardboard
- A 30-cm (1-ft) metal or wooden rod just less than 6 mm (¼ in) in diameter
- Water
- A pump with a needle (the kind you use for pumping up footballs)
- Plastic tubing to extend bicycle pump hose

To construct the rocket

1 TAPE YOUR STRAW to the exterior of the bottle. Make sure it is aligned with the centre of the bottle. You will use this to launch the rocket.

2 CUT FOUR ROCKET FINS out of cardboard and tape them to the outside of the bottle around the mouth. Be careful not to cover or compress the straw. The rocket will launch upside-down, so the mouth of the bottle will be the bottom of the rocket.

3 CREATE A NOSE CONE out of cardboard and tape it onto the top of the rocket (that is, the bottom of the bottle).

4 IF YOU WANT YOU CAN PAINT THE FINS, nose cone and bottle, but only lightly – the more weight there is on the bottle the harder it's going to be for it to fly really high.

To launch the rocket

1 FILL THE BOTTLE up to about halfway with water. The exact amount of water will affect how far your rocket will fly, so be prepared to experiment.

2 PUSH THE RUBBER STOPPER securely into the mouth of the bottle. Tape it down if need be to hold it in place, leaving the small hole at the centre of the stopper open. If you can't find a stopper with a hole, drill a hole through a wine-bottle cork and use that instead.

3 FIT A BICYCLE PUMP with about 3 m (10 ft) of extension tubing, fixing the pump needle at the end of the hose. If you don't have extension tubing, don't worry – just remember that whoever is pumping is going to get wet when the rocket takes off.

4 IN A FIELD, SINK THE ROD straight into the ground and slide the straw taped to the side of the rocket onto it. Make sure the rocket is pointing directly upwards.

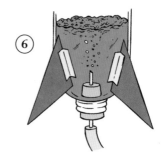

5 PUSH THE NEEDLE through the hole in the rubber stopper.

6 STAND WELL BACK and pump air into the bottle at a steady rate.

7 WHEN THE PRESSURE in the bottle gets high enough, the rocket will blast off in an explosion of water!

8 THE AMOUNT OF WATER in the bottle will determine how high or low the rocket will fly. Too much water makes the bottle too heavy, but too little water means not enough thrust. Experiment with less water to get your device to fly higher.

WARNING

Before launching, always make sure your rocket isn't pointing directly at anyone.

Cooking up slime

❦

No crazy science adventure would be complete without a slime-making project. It's disgusting, it gives your mum and sister the creeps, and it comes in handy around Hallowe'en . . . You can make this yourself in about 30 minutes, although it might be fun to have a lab assistant (you can call him 'Igor').

YOU WILL NEED
- A small bottle of white PVA glue
- Green food colouring (other colours are ok, but green is a great colour for slime!)
- Borax powder
- A jar
- A mixing bowl
- A spoon for stirring
- Water

STEPS

1 POUR THE ENTIRE BOTTLE of glue into a jar. Fill the empty glue bottle with water, shake it gently to mix up the last of the glue, and empty it into the jar.

2 STIR IN ABOUT FIVE DROPS of food colouring.

3 PUT ONE CUP OF WATER and of one teaspoon of borax powder in a mixing bowl. Empty the glue-water mixture in the jar into the water-borax mixture. Stir until the mix starts to become dough-like.

4 WHEN YOU CAN'T STIR ANY MORE, use your hands to knead the slime. It will become firmer and less sticky the more you knead it.

5 YOUR CREATION IS COMPLETE! When you've finished using it to scare your little sister, store the slime in an airtight container in the fridge or it will go mouldy.

Sending a secret message with invisible ink

❖

Invisible ink has been around for centuries as a way to send secret communications. It was used widely by both sides in the American Revolutionary War, for example. Sending blank pieces of paper might arouse suspicion, so the commanders would tell their agents and spies to write normal family letters, but to leave room between the lines and in the margins. They then used this space to write secret messages with invisible ink, or 'the Stain', as it was called. That way, if the letter fell into enemy hands, it would look like any other piece of correspondence and the plans it carried would stay secret.

How to write a secret message

You never know when you might need to pass secret communications yourself, away from the prying eyes of enemy spies, or your brother or sister, so here's how. This is an easy project which you can do by yourself in about five minutes – although it'll take longer if you plan to write a book with the stuff. Make sure you tell the intended reader of the secret letters how to reveal the invisible ink or your message won't get through.

YOU WILL NEED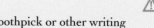

- The juice of one lemon (more if you plan to write a lot)
- A knife
- A small bowl
- A toothpick or other writing implement (i.e. cotton bud or quill pen)
- Paper

STEPS

1 CUT A LEMON IN HALF and squeeze the juice out into a bowl. This is your secret ink – simple as that.

2 DIP YOUR WRITING IMPLEMENT into the lemon juice and write your message. Put on two or three layers of juice to make the message easy to read when it's revealed.

3 TO AVOID ANY SUSPICION, use the old-fashioned method and write your secret message in the blank spaces of a conventional note. Post it or leave it at an agreed location for your contact to pick up.

How to reveal the secret message

There are two ways to reveal a message written in invisible ink: by light bulb, or by cabbage water.

1 HOLD THE NOTE UP TO A LIGHT BULB, or something else that gives off a low heat. Lightbulbs can burn the paper so don't hold it too close for too long! As it warms up, the invisible ink should turn brown and reveal your message.

2 YOU CAN ALSO REVEAL THE MESSAGE by spraying your note with a light mist of cabbage water. Simply cut a head of red cabbage into chunks, and boil them in a pan of water until the water turns a deep shade of purple. Let the water cool before putting it in a spray bottle and misting it gently over the paper. Where it touches the invisible ink, the message should slowly appear.

DID YOU KNOW? Government printers put secret marks in invisible ink on stamps, banknotes and other official documents. They use chemicals that are invisible in ordinary conditions, but which fluoresce (glow brightly) under ultra-violet light. Forgers may not know about the invisible writing, so forgeries can be detected simply by scanning the document with ultra-violet light and looking for the secret marks. If they don't show up, you can instantly tell the document is a fake.

Making paper

✦✦✦

People have been using some form of paper for thousands of years. That's partly because paper is made out of wood and plant fibres, both abundant natural resources. Nearly 5,000 years ago the Egyptians wrote on pages made from a reed called *papyrus*, which they pounded into flat sheets. The word 'papyrus' gave us our word 'paper'.

A few thousand years later, the Chinese wrote on strips of bamboo tied together, or on sheets of silk, but later switched to pages made from wood pulp like modern paper. And in the New World, Mayan civilizations in what is now Mexico used the inner bark of fig trees to make *amate*. They would boil the bark, then pound it with stones into thin sheets for them to write on.

When the Greeks built the massive Library of Alexandria in Egypt, around 300 B.C., they used up all the papyrus in Egypt filling its shelves. So they began to use parchment, a paper made out of calf- or sheepskin stretched out and dried. The use of parchment spread to other countries, and it was the paper of choice for many European civilizations for the next 1,000 years.

This project doesn't require any tree bark or stone pounding, fun as that may sound. It does require a little help, and probably the best part of one day to make the paper and another whole day to dry it.

YOU WILL NEED

- Paper scraps (newspaper, tissue paper, paper towels, paper bags, cards, etc.)
- A blender
- A sponge
- A piece of fine metal mesh (the kind used for window screening) a little bigger than your paper
- An old wooden picture frame the size of your piece of paper
- Staples or tacks and a hammer
- A basin or tub large enough to immerse the frame
- A bowl
- Cloths a little bigger than your paper will be
- Liquid starch
- A rolling pin

STEPS

1 TEAR YOUR SCRAP PAPER into small pieces and soak them in a bowl of hot water for at least 30 minutes.

2 ONCE ALL YOUR PAPER has been thoroughly soaked, fill a blender with equal parts soaked paper and warm water.

3 BLEND AT MEDIUM SPEED until you have a soupy mixture, and you can no longer see any bits of paper.

4 STAPLE THE MESH over one side of the wooden frame, and cut away the excess screen. In the paper-making business this is called a deckle.

5 FILL A BASIN or tub halfway with warm water and pour in your paper mixture.

6 STIR IN TWO TEASPOONS of starch (this prevents the finished paper from soaking up too much ink).

7 TAKE YOUR DECKLE and submerge it in the tub mesh side up, to get a thin but even layer of paper mixture on the screen.

8 LIFT THE DECKLE out of the water and let the excess water drip off. Use your fingers to push the paper gently down to squeeze out more water.

9 LAY A CLOTH ON A FLAT SURFACE and turn the deckle and the paper mixture gently over onto the cloth.

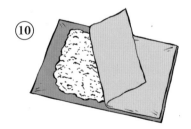

10 REMOVE THE DECKLE, leaving the flat paper mixture on the cloth. Cover the paper with a second cloth.

11 USING A ROLLING PIN, gently roll across the top cloth, to dry and flatten out your paper and to remove any bubbles that may have formed.

12 REMOVE THE TOP CLOTH and let your paper dry overnight. It should now be ready to write on!

13 REPEAT THE ABOVE PROCESS as many times as you like, to get a good number of sheets.

How to marble paper

To give your paper colour or texture, you can blend coloured construction paper, or bits of flowers or herbs into the recipe. Or you can get very elaborate designs surprisingly easily by marbling the finished paper using brightly coloured oil paints. Actually marbling the paper takes about 10 minutes. It'll take a bit longer for the paint to dry.

YOU WILL NEED

- Sheets of paper (preferably home-made)
- An assortment of oil paints
- Turpentine
- An empty plastic egg carton
- A pan large enough to put your paper in
- Dishwashing liquid
- Sticks for stirring paint (lolly sticks will do)
- Newspaper

STEPS

1 PREPARE A WORKSTATION by laying down sheets of newspaper – this can get messy! You'll want to put enough down to have room for drying the marbled sheets without them touching each other.

2 FILL THE PAN HALFWAY up with warm water and add a drop of dishwashing liquid. This will help the paints to disperse so you get more complex, interesting patterns on your marbled paper.

3 FILL EACH SECTION of an empty egg carton with a different coloured oil paint and thin each paint with a couple of drops of turpentine. If the paint's too thick, it'll just sit in lumps on the surface of your water and won't make interesting patterns on the paper.

4 USING A BRUSH OR A LOLLY STICK, drip paint on the surface of the water. Choose a few bright colours that'll look good on your paper. Because they're oil-based, the paints will float on the surface.

5 GENTLY SWIRL THE PAINTS on the water with a lolly stick to create patterns. Don't stir too much, or the paints will all mix together and you'll just get a brown mess.

6 BEND A SHEET OF PAPER into a 'U' shape and set the centre down on the surface of the paints and water. Then lay the sides gently down to touch the water. Do not submerge the paper – keep it floating on the surface.

7 USE A STICK TO LIFT ONE CORNER of the paper and remove it immediately from the pan – if you leave it too long, your paper will start to get wet and disintegrate.

8 THE OIL-PAINT SWIRLS should have transferred themselves to your paper. Repeat from step 6 with as many other sheets as you like.

9 LAY YOUR MARBLED PAPER face up on newspaper to dry. Give it at least an hour to make sure the patterns are fixed.

10 IF THE EDGES OF THE PAPER CURL UP as they dry, place the dried paper between two flat sheets of cloth and iron it over medium heat to flatten it out.

DID YOU KNOW? Marbling paper seems to have been invented in China in about the tenth century, and brought over to Europe through Iran and Turkey in the 1600s. It became very popular as the end papers for books (the pages that join the insides to the cover). Since no two marbled pages are ever identical, the exact pattern of marbling on the endpapers can be used to identify specific copies of rare books.

Growing a crystal

❖

Crystals have always had a special place in human culture. Many ancient civilizations used them in spiritual and healing ceremonies, because they thought crystals had magical or holy properties that could channel energy into their owners. The ancient Egyptians, for example, believed crystals could bring good health, protection and good fortune.

DID YOU KNOW? Diamonds are crystals. They're also the most valuable, the oldest and the hardest naturally occurring substance on earth. The largest rough diamond ever found was the Cullinan Diamond, which was discovered in 1905 in Africa. Uncut it weighed 3106.75 carats – roughly the size of a grapefruit. Soon after it was found, it was cut into a 530.2 carat gem called the Star of Africa, which is now part of the crown jewels of the British Royal Family.

You can grow your own crystals in your kitchen. Alum – a pickling powder that may be found in the spice aisle at the supermarket – makes great crystals. It takes about two days for a crystal to start forming and about two weeks for it to grow to a good size. The longer you wait, the bigger your crystal will get.

YOU WILL NEED

- 120 ml (½ cup) hot tap-water
- 30 g (2 ½ tbsp) alum
- 10 cm (4 in) of thread or fishing line
- A lolly stick
- 2 clean jars
- A long spoon
- A few sheets of paper towel
- An elastic band

STEPS

1 CAREFULLY RINSE OUT a jar. Boil water and pour 120 ml (½ cup) into the clean jar.

2 DISSOLVE THE ALUM POWDER in the water. You won't need all 2½ tablespoons, so pour in the alum a little at a time and stir until it dissolves. When the alum won't dissolve any more, the water is saturated and ready to start producing your crystals.

3 COVER THE JAR with a paper towel. Use the elastic band to keep the paper towel on tight. Let the jar sit in a dark place overnight.

4 THE NEXT DAY, you will see a layer of small crystals on the bottom of the jar. One of these will be the 'seed' for the second half of the experiment.

5 POUR THE ALUM SOLUTION into a second jar, making sure to keep the crystals in the first jar. Fish the largest crystal out of the jar with a spoon.

6 TIE FISHING LINE AROUND THE CRYSTAL – this bit's tricky. You can use sewing thread instead of nylon fishing line, but crystals don't adhere to nylon, so you can get a single bigger, better crystal if you use nylon.

7 TIE THE OTHER END around the middle of a lolly stick, making sure the line is long enough for the crystal to be submerged into the alum solution without touching the bottom of the jar.

8 LOWER THE CRYSTAL into the alum solution in the second jar, resting the lolly stick on the mouth of the jar. Cover the jar with a paper towel.

9 CHECK ON THE CRYSTAL every day and watch it grow. When it's big enough, carefully snip off the fishing line and put the crystal on display.

10 EXPERIMENT WITH OTHER SUBSTANCES that dissolve in water, like salt, and see if you can persuade crystals to grow.

Making an electromagnet

There are two types of magnet: permanent and electrical ones. Permanent magnetism occurs naturally in some rocks with metallic properties. It's also possible to permanently magnetize metal – that's the most common type of permanent magnet, which can be found on refrigerators throughout the world.

Electromagnets are different. They're made when a piece of metal become magnetised as an electric current flows through it. Electromagnets are also very common – they just don't end up on your refrigerator. The standard ones are made from coils of wire wrapped around a metal core. When electricity is passed through the wire, a magnetic field is generated in the coil that turns the core into one big magnet. When the electricity is turned off, so is the magnetic field, which is what makes electromagnets so useful. You can find them in all kinds of devices including electric guitars, electric motors and door bells, as well as loudspeakers and computer hard drives.

Researchers at Florida State University in the USA claim to have the strongest electromagnet in the world. It is 4.8 m (16 ft) tall, weighs 13.6 tonnes (15 tons) and has a magnetic force 420,000 times stronger than the Earth's magnetic field. The magnet helps with chemical and biomedical research by slowing down tiny particles like atoms, which normally move very fast, so that scientists can study them. Compasses work because the needle lines up with the Earth's natural magnetic field, running north to south. But a normal fridge magnet has a stronger magnetic force than the Earth's magnetic field. That's why compass needles have to be so small and light – so they can respond to the Earth's pull. In fact, you can use a fridge magnet to make a compass needle point south!

YOU WILL NEED

- A 7.5-cm (3-in) long iron nail
- 90 cm (3 ft) of low-voltage insulated copper wire
- A new D battery (1.5V)
- Masking tape
- A penknife
- Paper clips

STEPS

1 WRAP THE COPPER WIRE tightly around the nail, leaving 20 cm (8 in) of wire free at each end. In theory, the more coils you have the stronger the magnetic field is going to be, so keep them close to each other. But be careful not to overlap the coils.

2 USING A PENKNIFE, remove about 2.5 cm (1 in) of the plastic coating from each end of the wire to leave the metal exposed.

3 TAPE ONE EXPOSED END of the wire to each end of your battery.

4 AS SOON AS BOTH ENDS ARE CONNECTED, your nail will be magnetized and you can use it to pick up the paper clips.

5 TO DE-MAGNETIZE THE NAIL, remove one wire from the battery. Any paper clips attached to the nail should fall off.

6 WITH THE BATTERY CONNECTED, put your nail on a piece of paper. Find a magnetic compass, and try putting it in different places around the nail. Draw a little arrow on the paper at each place to show the direction the compass needle is pointing. The shapes of the arrows will show the shape of the magnetic field you have created.

DID YOU KNOW? The connection between electricity and magnets is very important. You can turn a piece of iron into a magnet by passing an electric current through it, but you can also generate an electric current in a piece of iron by surrounding it with moving magnets. Generators in power stations contain very large magnets, which spin round a metal core to create an electric current.

Building an erupting volcano

Volcanoes are one of Nature's most frightening and exciting phenomena. They are essentially valves on the Earth's surface, which release pressurised gas and molten rock from deep underground in eruptions that can be catastrophic. So why not build your own?

DID YOU KNOW? Mount Saint Helens in the United States and Mount Vesuvius in Italy are two of the best-known volcanoes in the world. They are both stratovolcanoes, built up layer upon layer by lava and ash that has covered their sides over the years. Stratovolcanoes are also prone to periodic and explosive eruptions. Mount Vesuvius erupted in 79 CE, burying the Roman towns of Herculaneum and Pompeii under a deep layer of ash and killing many of their inhabitants. When Mount Saint Helens erupted in 1980, the entire peak of the mountain was blown into dust and ash, reducing hundreds of square kilometres to wasteland.

By simulating an eruption, you can see how lava flows down the sides of a mountain. It's a dramatic experiment, and it's also good fun. Always wear protective eyewear as the 'eruption' can bubble and splatter. It'll take two hours or more to build the volcano, overnight for it to dry and another hour to paint it. Preparing the eruption takes 10 minutes.

To construct the volcano

YOU WILL NEED
- A 90- x 90-cm (3- x 3-ft) sheet of plywood
- A large plastic bottle
- Masking tape
- Newspaper
- Flour
- Water
- Paint

STEPS

1 CUT OFF THE TOP THIRD of the plastic bottle and tape the bottom section to the middle of your square of plywood.

2 LOOSELY CRUMPLE NEWSPAPER into balls and place them around the bottle in the rough shape of a volcano, leaving the mouth of the plastic bottle open. Use masking tape to hold all the newspaper in place.

3 MAKE PAPIER-MÂCHÉ PASTE by mixing one part flour with one part water and stirring until the mixture's smooth.

4 CUT LONG STRIPS OF NEWSPAPER and soak them in papier-mâché paste. Get them good and wet, but not so soggy that they fall apart.

5 PLACE WET STRIPS OF PAPER all around the volcano working from top to bottom. Make a lip around the top of the plastic bottle but don't cover it over – this is where the eruption will come from. You can put on up to four layers of papier-mâché.

6 MAKE SURE YOU INCLUDE some realistic lava channels and rocky outcrops. You could even direct the lava down one side at this stage by making ridges and valleys. Get creative!

7 LET THE PAPIER-MÂCHÉ DRY overnight, so it's solid and ready to paint. Don't try and paint it when it's wet, or it'll fall apart.

8 PAINT THE VOLCANO the next day in realistic rock colours. Don't forget to paint on some red lava flows!

9 PUT MODEL TREES, or tiny action figures on the side of the volcano, or make some little houses out of cardboard and paint them in brick or stone colours. Or add dinosaurs for a prehistoric feel!

10 LET THE PAINT dry completely, and you're ready to prepare for the first stages of the eruption.

To make your volcano erupt

YOU WILL NEED

- 60 ml (¼ cup) of water
- 15 ml (1 tbsp) of bicarbonate of soda
- 60 ml (¼ cup) of vinegar
- A few drops of red food colouring
- A few drops of washing up liquid
- A small square of tissue paper
- Protective eyewear

1 PUT ON your protective eyewear.

2 POUR THE RIGHT MEASUREMENTS of water, detergent, food colouring, and vinegar into the plastic bottle at the centre of the volcano and stir it all together.

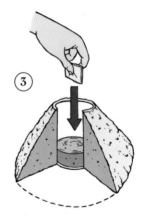

3 WRAP THE BICARBONATE OF SODA in a square of tissue and drop it into the bottle. Stand back!

4 THE MIXTURE IN THE BOTTLE will begin to foam and bubble up over the top of the volcano and down the sides.

DID YOU KNOW? The mixture works because bicarbonate of soda gives off carbon dioxide when it comes into contact with the vinegar-water mixture. (It does the same in contact with plain water, just a bit more slowly – the gas is what makes cakes rise while they're cooking.) The washing up liquid catches the gas in bubbles, so it makes a thick foam that flows like lava over the edges of the crater and down the sides of the mountain. The food colouring is just to give your eruption a good, fiery colour!

Crushing a drinks can using only water

❦ ❦

You don't have to travel to Niagara Falls or rent a high-power water sprayer for this to work. Everything you need is in the kitchen. By changing the air pressure inside a can you'll be able to crush it with just the weight of some water in a bucket.

YOU WILL NEED ⚠

- A normal soft drink can
- A cooker
- Metal tongs

- A bucket of water large enough to completely submerge the can

STEPS

1 FILL A BUCKET with cold water and put it next to the cooker.

2 POUR JUST ENOUGH WATER into a can to cover the bottom. Holding the can with a pair of tongs, heat it over a gas burner. This drives the air out of the can and replaces it with hot water vapour.

3 WHEN THE WATER in the can begins to boil, lift it off the stove and submerge it, mouth-end down, in the bucket of water.

4 THE CAN WILL IMMEDIATELY FOLD IN ON ITSELF! The heated water vapour inside the can will condense in the cold water, causing the pressure inside the can to drop so that the water pressure outside will crush it.

WARNING

Be careful when moving the can around, as it will get very hot.

Putting a boiled egg in a bottle

❖

This is one of those brilliant science experiments that's almost like a magic trick. Try this at your little brother's birthday party to impress his friends. What you'll be doing is forcing a hard-boiled egg through the neck of a glass bottle, first into the bottle and then out. Most people think the only way to do this is to scramble the egg, but not so. Here's what you need to do:

Putting the egg in the bottle

By heating the inside of a bottle you expand the air contained in it. As the air cools off, it creates a vacuum that sucks the egg through without breaking it. It takes about 20 minutes to boil, cool and peel an egg, so prepare this beforehand. It only takes two minutes to get the egg in the bottle, and another five minutes to get it out.

YOU WILL NEED
- A hard-boiled egg
- A glass bottle with a neck and mouth not less than half the width of the egg
- Three matches

STEPS

1 BOIL AN EGG FOR 15 MINUTES until it's hard all the way through, then run it under cold water until it's cool to the touch.

2 PEEL THE SHELL OFF, making sure you don't damage the exterior of the egg. If you can leave the membrane inside the shell intact, so much the better.

3 WHEN THE EGG IS READY to go, gather the rest of your ingredients together, and make sure you have an audience.

4 LIGHT THREE MATCHES and carefully drop them in the bottom of the bottle and wait three seconds.

5 PLACE THE EGG UPRIGHT on top of the mouth of the bottle.

6 WATCH AS THE EGG slips down the neck and into your bottle!

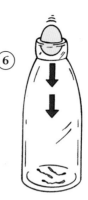

How to get the egg out

YOU WILL NEED
- A boiled egg in a bottle
- An Alka-Seltzer tablet
- Water

1 POUR 2.5 CM (1 IN) of tap water into the bottom of your bottle, alongside the egg and burnt-up matches.

2 BREAK UP AN ALKA-SELTZER TABLET and drop the pieces into your bottle with the water.

3 CAREFULLY UP-END THE BOTTLE so that the egg acts as a seal at the base of the neck of your bottle.

4 PRESSURE CREATED BY THE GAS fizzing off the Alka-Seltzer tablet should push the egg out.

DID YOU KNOW? Alka-Seltzer, like the bicarbonate of soda in our volcano (see page 88), gives off carbon dioxide when it comes into contact with water. Chemists designed it to do this so it would dissolve quickly. Because the egg is blocking the bottle neck, the gas given off by the tablet cannot escape, so the pressure inside the bottle increases. The build-up of pressure pushes the egg back out of the bottle – abracadabra!

Making a telephone

Most people think telephones are complex machines, but the land-line phone in your house is one of the simplest devices around. In fact, the technology hasn't changed too much since it was invented in the 1870s (although mobile phone and wireless technology is a different story). Essentially, when a person speaks into a phone their voice vibrates a membrane. Those sound vibrations are transferred along the phone line to another phone where they are recreated identically through another membrane that acts as a speaker. In a phone line, the vibrations are carried electrically, but you can recreate this technique physically using string telephones.

YOU WILL NEED
- Two paper cups
- A long piece of string
- Two paper clips
- A sewing needle

STEPS

1 USE THE NEEDLE to poke a hole through the centre at the bottom of each of your two cups.

2 PUSH ONE END OF THE STRING up through each hole, and tie it to a paper clip so the string doesn't slip out of the cup.

3 GIVE ONE CUP TO A FRIEND and get far enough apart so that the string is stretched out taut between you.

4 TALK AND LISTEN into the cups. Vibrations from your voice should be carried along the string to the cup at the other end.

Building a periscope

❧ ❧

Boys can never have enough spying tools. One that's
easy to make on your own is a periscope that can allow you to
sneakily see over and around walls without sticking your head
into plain sight. You can attach one to your tree house, so you
can see anyone underneath it without giving yourself away by
looking over the side. Or you can use one in a game of hide and
seek, to secretly watch for the seeker from your hiding place.
This project shouldn't take more than an hour.

DID YOU KNOW? You've probably seen periscopes used on submarines
in films to allow the crew to spy on ships without having to come up to the
surface. But did you know they're also used by tank commanders to see out
of their vehicles without having to leave the safety of their armour? They
were also used in World War I by soldiers in the trenches, to see over the
battlefield without putting themselves in danger from enemy snipers.

YOU WILL NEED
- 2-l(1-gall) paper milk cartons
- Two mirrors small enough to fit
  inside the cartons
- Tape
- Scissors

STEPS

1 WASH OUT YOUR MILK CARTONS thoroughly, so your periscope doesn't get too
smelly to use. Then cut off the tops of both containers with a pair of scissors, to
give you two deep cardboard boxes.

2 PUT THE MIRRORS IN PLACE at the bottom of each milk carton. They should be tilted over one corner, so that one side of each mirror rests on the bottom of the container and one side rests on the wall of the container. Tape them loosely into place – we'll secure them properly in a moment.

3 CUT A WIDE WINDOW into each carton opposite each mirror.

4 HOLD ONE CONTAINER upside down onto the other so that the windows you just cut are on opposite sides of the periscope. This allows you to look in through the back at the bottom and look out through the front at the top.

5 NOW'S THE TIME TO ADJUST THE MIRRORS. Look into the bottom of the periscope while holding the top with your hand. Make sure the angles of the mirrors line up with each other so you can see clearly through the top window. If they don't, adjust one of the mirrors until you can see clearly. When you've got it right, secure the mirrors permanently in place with more tape.

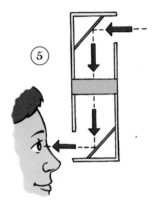

6 TAPE THE TWO MILK CARTONS together, holding them carefully in place so the two mirrors stay in line.

7 NOW YOU CAN DECORATE your new periscope. Work out where you're going to be using it most and colour it so it'll be camouflaged: dark green for a treehouse, light brown for dusty ground, and so on.

DID YOU KNOW? The reason we can see an object is that light bounces off it into our eyes. By angling the mirrors inside an enclosed space, we are allowing light to bounce from one mirror to the next and into our eye. Modern periscopes use optical fibres for mirrors – these are rods of special plastic that reflect light internally all along their length. Because they're very small, they can be slipped through keyholes to spy inside, or even threaded inside the body so doctors can inspect organs or the insides of veins.

Levitating a ping-pong ball

❧

Levitating magic or just good science? Here's another experiment that you could wear a red cape and black top hat while doing, even though it's entirely based on solid physics.

The reason a ping-pong ball floats in one place instead of flying up and away or dropping is the same reason aeroplanes can fly. It's called Bernoulli's Principle, after a Swiss scientist who discovered that moving air exerts less pressure than still air. Wings let huge metal aeroplanes fly because, as the plane is driving down the runway, air rushing over the top of the wing exerts less pressure than the air under the wing. The air under the wing essentially pushes the plane into the sky. A ping-pong ball in a stream of wind from a hair dryer will stay in one place because the still air above and on the sides is pushing on the ball, holding it in the stream.

This is one of the easiest experiments to perform but it has a big payoff. You won't need any help and you can get started by plugging in and turning on an ordinary hairdryer.

YOU WILL NEED

- A hairdryer
- A ping-pong ball

STEPS

1 STAND UP AND TURN THE HAIRDRYER ON at a cool setting, only blowing gently for starters.

2 POINT THE HAIRDRYER UP and place the ping-pong ball in the air stream coming out of the hairdryer. It will float!

3 TRY TURNING THE HAIRDRYER to higher settings and watch the ball raise slowly into the air.

4 TURN THE HAIRDRYER OFF and the ball falls to the ground. If you really want to show off, catch it as it comes down!

Simulating a tornado

Tornadoes are one of the world's scariest weather events. They are funnel-shaped clouds of swirling wind that extend all the way to the ground, where they can lift houses off their foundations and send cars flying through the air up to 90 m (300 ft) away. They occur when the wind in a thunder cloud moves in different directions at different levels, causing fierce circular air currents. People have come up with various names for tornadoes including twisters, Devil's tails and stovepipes. Those who investigate tornadoes by either driving or flying very close to them are called storm chasers.

Though you wouldn't want to get close to a real tornado, you can pretend to be a storm chaser by creating a tornado using coloured water in a bottle. You can do this project by yourself, and it shouldn't take more than 30 minutes to construct.

DID YOU KNOW? When a tornado touches down, the fast-swirling winds carve a very clear path along the ground. Anything in that path is usually destroyed while the areas outside the path look as though nothing happened. Tornado paths have been measured anywhere from 2 m (7 ft) to 1.5 km (1 mile) wide. The most violent tornado ever recorded hit parts of Missouri, Illinois and Indiana in 1925. It traveled 352 km (219 miles), lasted three and a half hours, and caused the deaths of nearly 700 people.

Where tornadoes occur over the sea, they create water spouts: huge, swirling columns of water reaching up into the sky. These can move very fast across the sea, and can be very dangerous to unwary boats. You might also have heard of the rare and mysterious phenomenon of fish or frogs raining down from the sky. Scientists think this might be caused by tornadoes or water spouts sucking small animals up into the air, carrying them along in strong air currents high above the ground and dropping them back down many miles away.

YOU WILL NEED

- Two large plastic bottles
- Water
- Insulating tape
- Scissors

- A ruler
- Paper towel
- A pencil
- Blue food colouring

STEPS

1 HALF FILL ONE of the bottles with water, and add a few drops of food colouring to help you see what happens.

2 CUT A LENGTH OF TAPE large enough to cover the mouth of the bottle. Tape it down over the mouth of the bottle.

3 USING THE SHARPENED TIP of a pencil, pierce the middle of the tape to create a hole about the width of the pencil.

4 ALIGN THE MOUTH of the second bottle with the mouth of the water-filled bottle and tape the two mouths securely together with more tape.

5 TURN THE TWO BOTTLES OVER so that the water-filled bottle is on top. Quickly swirl the bottles in a circle several times, and set them down – still with the full bottle on top – on a flat surface.

6 WATCH AS A FUNNEL APPEARS in the top bottle. As the water flows, it'll develop into a miniature tornado inside the bottle.

DID YOU KNOW? Technically this swirling effect is known as a 'vortex', and it's formed whenever liquids or gases flow from an area of high pressure to an area of low pressure. Studies like these help scientists to understand not only extreme weather like tornadoes and water spouts, but also hurricanes and thunderstorms.

Chapter Four

Building

WE'VE EXPLORED, HUNTED AND EXPERIMENTED.
Now let's build something. From folding up a
paper aeroplane to constructing an igloo, building
things is a great way to spend an afternoon.
Plus, you can keep what you build forever.

✦

A pinhole camera isn't just fun to make: the
images you can capture will last a lifetime.
You can even build things to help on your other
adventures. A radio, for example, can let you
eavesdrop on passing aircraft while pretending
you're a World War II spy. Follow these easy steps,
and whatever you build, build it to last.

Paper aeroplanes

❧

One of the easiest and best things to make on a rainy day is a
paper aeroplane. All you really need is a sheet of paper – unless
you plan to make an entire air force, which, by the way, might
be fun!

Over the years, inventors have learned a lot about flight by making model
aeroplanes. Some say that Leonardo DaVinci invented the model aeroplane in the
fifteenth century – about 400 years before the Wright brothers made the historic
first flight in a real plane.

Longest flying plane

YOU WILL NEED
- A rectangular sheet of paper

STEPS

1 FOLD THE PAPER in half lengthwise to create a crease, then unfold it and lay it
flat. Fold the paper in half widthwise to create another crease perpendicular to
(making a cross with) the first crease.

2 UNFOLD THE PAPER AND LAY IT FLAT. Turn it so the short side is towards you,
and fold the top of the paper down so it meets the widthwise crease.

3 FOLD THE CORNERS on that side in so they meet at the lengthwise centre crease,
then fold the tip of the plane down onto itself to make a blunt nose for the plane.

4 FOLD THE PLANE IN HALF along the lengthwise centre crease.

5 NEXT MAKE THE WINGS. Fold one side down then flip the plane over and fold
the other side down. Only leave about 1 cm (½ in) on the body of the plane to
hold onto.

6 TAKE YOUR PLANE OUTSIDE and see how it flies!

Fastest flying plane

YOU WILL NEED
● A rectangular sheet of paper

STEPS

1 FOLD THE PAPER IN HALF LENGTHWISE to create a crease.

2 UNFOLD IT AND LAY IT FLAT. Make a point by folding one corner in to align with the centre crease, then doing the same with the opposite corner.

3 SHARPEN THE POINT by folding each corner in again, on top of the corners you just folded. Do this on both sides, and align the folded corners with the centre crease once again. Now fold the paper in half at the centre crease.

4 NOW MAKE THE WINGS. Fold one side down so that it's about 1 cm (½ in) above the centre fold near the point, but about 2.5 cm (1 in) above the centre fold in the rear. Turn the plane over and repeat this on the other side.

5 ATTACH A PAPER CLIP TO THE FRONT NOSE. This adds balance and will protect the nose when the plane rockets through the air and hits the ground. Now prepare for take-off!

If the plane dives down when it flies, fold the back tips of the wings up slightly. Decrease the angle of the rear wing folds if the plane wants to fly up. Adding a second paper clip to the nose can help with this problem as well.

DID YOU KNOW? The world record for the longest time in the air for a paper aeroplane is 27.6 seconds. The record for the longest distance is 59 m (193 ft) – more than the width of a football field.

Model boats

❧❧

If you can make a plane out of paper you can make a boat out of paper, too. Paper boats can be great fun after a heavy rain, when you can often find small but fast streams of water running in the street.

This project shouldn't take more than 10 minutes. The first one can be a bit tricky, but once you get in the swing of things you'll have an armada in no time.

> **YOU WILL NEED**
> - A rectangular sheet of heavyweight paper

STEPS

1 FOLD THE PAPER IN HALF lengthwise to make a centre crease.

2 OPEN IT OUT and fold it in half widthwise.

3 WITH THE FOLD AT THE TOP, fold down the corners so that they meet at the centre crease, giving you two triangles with a long rectangle underneath.

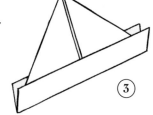

4 AT THE BOTTOM, fold one side of the paper up and over the bottom of the triangles. Then fold the corners of that strip of paper over the edge of the triangles.

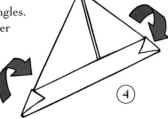

5 TURN THE PAPER OVER and fold the strip of paper up on that side. Now you should have what looks like a hat.

6 HOLD THE HAT UPSIDE DOWN, put your thumbs on the inside and pull it open. The two ends of the hat will come together – press them flat and you will be left with a diamond.

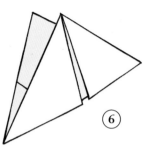

7 AT THE END WHERE YOUR DIAMOND OPENS, fold each side down so that you're left with a triangle.

8 PLACE YOUR THUMBS INSIDE that triangle as you did the hat earlier and pull it open until the ends meet and you've formed another diamond.

9 TURN THE DIAMOND UPSIDE DOWN and pull the sides away from the middle to form a boat with a triangle mast.

10 TAKE IT TO A STREAM or puddle and watch it sail!

Racing paper boats is great fun. After a rainstorm, take a few friends with a paper boat each and find a good-sized puddle. Just put your boats in at one end, and blow or fan them to the other end as fast as you can. Or find a stream, put all the boats in at the same place, and see which one reaches the finishing line first. Experiment with different designs and different sizes to see which ones go fastest. Here's a tip: remember that bigger boats will catch the wind better and so be blown along faster, but smaller boats are less likely to get stuck on twigs or other obstacles in a stream.

You can also decorate your boat by painting it, or by marbling the paper before you start to fold (see page 80). Painting it with an oil-based paint can also help your boat to last longer before getting soggy and sinking. Why not set up teams of boats in different colours, so you know who to cheer during the race?

DID YOU KNOW? The largest ever fleet of paper boats was made in Germany in 1980. It had over 13,000 craft and filled a swimming pool!

A sledge

❦❦❦

With winter comes snow and a whole new type of adventure.
If you're not building an igloo or skating, you'll want to ride the
powder like an Arctic explorer. In other words, you'll want a
sledge. Nothing gets you from A to B faster when the ground is
thick with freshly fallen snow.

If it doesn't snow where you are – or you want to use your sledge in summer – you
can still slide on a flat-bottomed sledge down smooth grassy or sandy slopes. Only
problem is falling hurts a little more than onto snow! This is an advanced project
so you'll need some help and a few tools. You might even need a trip to the DIY
shop. You can cut all the wood you need from a single large sheet of plywood. The
whole thing will probably take you about two days.

YOU WILL NEED

- 0.6- x 1.2-m (2- x 4-ft),
  2.5-cm- (1-in-) thick sheet of
  plywood (top board)
- A saw
- Sandpaper
- 2.5-cm- (1-in-) wide chisel or
  router with 2.5-cm- (1-in-) bit
- Two 0.3- x 1.2-m (1- x 4-ft),
  2.5-cm- (1-in-) thick plywood
  (runners)
- Wood glue

- At least eight 5-cm (2-in) screws
- A screwdriver
- Four angle irons 15 cm (6 in) on
  each side, with at least four 0.5-cm
  (¼-in) wide bolt holes
- A pencil
- Drill with 0.5-cm (¼-in) bit
- At least 16 3-cm (1½-in-) long,
  0.5-cm (¼-in) wide bolts with
  plenty of washers and nuts
- 0.5 m (2 ft) of rope

STEPS

1 TAKE THE TOP BOARD and cut off the corners of one end with a saw. Round off
the corners where you've cut with sandpaper to make a semicircle which will be
the front of your sledge.

2 USE SANDPAPER TO ROUND OFF the back corners of the top board while you're there – rounded corners make falling off less painful.

3 USE A CHISEL OR ROUTER to create two 2.5-cm- (1-in-) wide, 0.5-cm (¼-in) deep grooves along the length of the top board, about 3 cm (1½ in) in from the sides. The two runners will fit into these grooves.

4 STACK THE TWO RUNNERS on top of each other and cut off the top right and bottom left corners.

5 SAND THE CUT CORNERS on both runners to make a smooth curve. This will run along the snow.

6 PLACE A THREAD OF WOOD GLUE along the top edge of each runner and fit them into the grooves on the top board. Secure the runners in place by drilling screws down into them through the top board.

7 TURN THE SLEDGE UPSIDE DOWN and lay the angle irons – iron strips bent at a right angle – in the corner between the runner and the bottom of the sledge. Use two angle irons for each runner, one at the front and one at the back. Use a pencil to mark the location of the bolt holes.

8 REMOVE THE ANGLE IRONS and drill holes all the way through the top board and runners where you have marked.

9 SECURE THE ANGLE IRONS in place with bolts to hold the runners securely in place. Use washers on both sides of the board.

10 DRILL A HOLE IN THE VERY FRONT of your sledge, and loop the rope through it so you've got something to hold onto while you ride.

11 DECORATE YOUR SLEDGE with paint and you're ready to go!

For a sturdier structure, take your finished sledge to a blacksmith and have metal runners fitted over the wooden ones – that'll protect them from unexpected rocks lurking beneath the snow. You can also coat the whole structure in waterproof lacquer or polyurethane to keep water out of the wood and stop it rotting.

An igloo

Igloos are buildings made out of snow blocks. They are the traditional homes for the Inuit people of Canada and Alaska. Some people might think the Inuit build with ice and snow because they like to be cold, but in fact snow has very good insulating qualities, because it holds a lot of air. That means when the air outside an igloo is -35°C (-40°F) the inside of an igloo can be a toasty 16°C (60°F), even without a fire. The warmth inside an igloo comes from body heat.

Building an igloo is surprisingly easy to do. You just need to have the right kind of snow and lots of it. You might get someone tall, like your dad, to help with the very top, which can be tricky to reach. This can take some time to build so set aside an entire afternoon.

When an igloo is built correctly, a fully grown man can stand on top of the dome without it caving in. The Inuit bring a small lamp inside their igloos to melt the inside of the walls slightly and make them turn into ice to help reinforce the strength of the dome. Whenever you're sitting on cold ground or snow, your body temperature is going to drop because the ground draws the heat away. Try to sit on a raised platform or chair to stay warm inside your igloo.

YOU WILL NEED
- Lots of dry, very hard snow
- A saw
- A snow shovel
- Waterproof, insulated gloves

Steps

1 FIND A LARGE SUPPLY of dry, hard snow – you want unbroken ice crystals in the snow if possible.

2 CUT BLOCKS FROM THE SNOW. Each block should be 90 cm (3 ft) long, 40 cm (15 in) high and 20 cm (8 in) deep.

3 **AS YOU CUT THE BLOCKS,** begin arranging them in an upwards-sloping spiral around yourself. You will be working from the inside of the dome. Shape the first block so that it slants upwards and work your way around. The hole you're making as you cut the blocks will become the floor of the igloo. Make the initial circle 2 m (6 ft) in diameter.

4 **AS YOU BUILD THE WALLS UP,** shape each block with your snow saw so that they all slant slightly upwards and lean slightly inwards to form a dome shape. Don't worry about the front door just yet.

5 **WHEN YOU GET NEAR THE TOP** and there isn't any more room to stack blocks, cut a hole at ground level for the front door. It should be no more than 60 cm (2 ft) high. You may have to dig snow out and create a short tunnel.

6 **CLOSE OFF THE TOP OF THE IGLOO** by cutting a block of snow in the shape of the hole. Make it slightly larger than the hole. Place it on top of the igloo, then go inside and use your snow saw to cut and shape the top block so that it drops snugly into the hole.

7 **CUT FOUR MORE BLOCKS** and lean them teepee-fashion over the entrance tunnel. This tunnel will keep wind and snow out of the igloo and will also help funnel cold air out of the igloo.

8 GO BACK INSIDE THE IGLOO and cut two 8-cm (3-in) ventilation holes in opposite sides of the igloo dome at about waist height. This also allows cold air to escape, while the warm air gets trapped under the dome.

If you live in an area with warm winters, that doesn't mean you can't have some sort of igloo. Some people have successfully built sand igloos at the beach, but that's an inexact science where luck plays as much of a role as the building material. If you try this out, be sure and get the right mix of sand and water, and start with a small igloo first in case it collapses and you end up buried.

WARNING

Although it will be warmer inside the igloo than outside, you will still need to wear warm clothing and use a winter sleeping bag if you want to spend the night without getting cold!

If you live in the desert, you might try adobe or mud brick igloos. The Native Americans used to create mud bricks out of *caliche*, a fine dirt found across the southwest United States. They would make a mix of mud, straw and water, pack it into lots of brick-sized wooden moulds and bake the mixture in the sun for a few days. Whole houses were built using this technique.

If you can't get hold of sand or *caliche*, there's always a papier mâché igloo. Make an igloo shape out of chicken wire and cover it in strips of newspaper soaked in paste made from flour and water. (See page 87 for more information on papier mâché.) With a bit of white paint and a little imagination, this can make quite a cozy igloo substitute for the summer months. And unlike the snow igloo, this version will never melt – until it rains!

DID YOU KNOW? Although you might think all igloos are made from snow, the big ones often have a tent inside. Snow is a very good insulator, so piling it round the outsides of your tent actually helps to keep heat in!

A terrarium

✥ ✥

Want to build your own world complete with a self-contained
weather system? Build a terrarium! Terraria are enclosed glass
containers filled with soil and plants. Since they're sealed up,
water inside condenses on the sides and top of the glass and runs
back down into the soil – automatic rain! You hardly ever have
to water, but you do get to watch the plants grow from seeds
to grown-ups.

To make a terrarium you can start with a simple jar. Bigger ecosystems can be
made in aquarium tanks, and can include tarantulas, lizards, frogs or other
creatures. Once you find all the ingredients the project will take an hour to do,
and you can have plants happily growing in a couple of weeks.

YOU WILL NEED

- A large glass jar with a wide
  opening and a metal lid
- Clumps or sheets of peat moss
- Long tweezers or tongs that can
  fit inside the jar opening
- Gravel
- Potting soil
- Small plants that like humid
  environments
- A funnel
- A screwdriver

STEPS

1 LINE THE BOTTOM of the jar with peat moss – this will hold any excess water,
like a sponge. Scatter a layer of gravel over the moss – this is to help water drain
down through to the peat moss.

2 ON TOP OF THE GRAVEL, PUT DOWN A LAYER of potting soil for your plants to
grow in. The moss-gravel-soil layers should be at least 7.5 cm (3 in) thick
in total.

3 **PLANT SEEDLINGS OR PLANTS IN THE JAR.** How many plants you put in will depend on how big your jar is. You don't want it to be too crowded. Use long tweezers or tongs to make small holes and to lower plants into the jar. Cover their roots and tamp soil loosely around the plants. If you're sowing seeds, spread soil lightly over the top.

4 **WATER** the plants lightly – about 100 ml (½ cup) of water should be enough. If your plants get too wet, the soil will turn to marsh and nothing will grow except mould.

5 **USE A SCREWDRIVER** or other sharp device to poke three or four small holes in the jar lid. Terraria need ventilation so mould doesn't grow inside. Screw the lid onto the jar.

6 **PLACE THE TERRARIUM** in a well-lit place near a window, but not in direct sunlight, as that can burn the plants inside.

7 **WATCH YOUR PLANTS GROW!** If you want to add more life, find a few insects in your back garden that eat plants and settle them in. Be careful not to have too many, though, or they'll eat faster than your plants can grow!

8 **WHEN YOUR PLANTS GROW** right up to the top of the jar, you can cut off the tips to slow them down a bit. This will also make them grow more bushy, so they fill the jar without growing out through the air holes.

9 **EVERY FEW MONTHS,** scrape off the top layer of potting soil and replace it with fresh stuff, to keep your plants nourished.

Plants need four things to grow: air, water, sunlight and nutrients from the soil. The jar acts as a miniature greenhouse, letting in light while trapping heat and water. The holes on the top let air in and the potting soil provides nutrients. All you have to do is make sure it doesn't get too hot and dry out, or too wet so that your plants start to rot. All in all, it's a pretty good place to be if you're a plant!

It's not such a good place for animals, though, which don't always like things as warm and moist as plants do. Your pet hamster, for example, definitely won't be happy in there! It's best just to leave it to the insects to explore the mysteries of your miniature jungle.

A flint axe

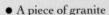

It's amazing to think about our primitive ancestors building their houses with tools made out of rocks. Not only did they use rocks as hammers, but they also made them into axes to cut down trees. It may sound as though it would take weeks to chop a tree down with just a stone, but that's exactly what Stone Age people did – and they had secret techniques to make their rocks as sharp as metal axes. The only difference is that they didn't last as long. But since no one had discovered iron yet, a rock was the best they could do. Archaeologists have found Stone-Age flint axes buried all around the world.

This is either an easy project or a not-so-easy one, depending on what kind of stone you can find. If you can locate one that's flat and sharp on one end, then you've got a great head start. Otherwise, you may have to try to shape the stone yourself using – you guessed it – other rocks. This technique is known as 'knapping' and has been used by humans for tens of thousands of years. The best rocks for sharpening are pieces of flint, which is a kind of shale that flakes easily into very sharp edges.

YOU WILL NEED

- A straight, 60-cm (2-ft) long piece of hardwood, about the circumference of your wrist or a little smaller
- A flint stone
- A piece of granite
- Twine (or leather straps, to be more authentic)
- Eye protection

STEPS

1 FIND A FLAT PIECE OF FLINT with one side sharpened into a point. If you can't find a suitable rock, use a lump of granite to shape a large piece of flint.

2 **PUT YOUR GOGGLES ON.** Hit the flint at an angle until one side splits away, leaving a sharp edge. If the rock is not flat, try to shape rounded grooves into the sides of the stone where it'll fit into the stick.

3 **SPLIT A STRAIGHT LENGTH** of hardwood down the middle for about 15 cm (6 in). You can do this using your newly sharpened piece of flint.

WARNING

Knapping stones creates sharp splinters that can fly off into your face. Always wear eye protection. Be careful when you're using the axe – make sure there's nobody standing nearby in case bits fly off or the axe head comes loose.

4 **NOW WEDGE IN THE AXE** head into the split.

5 **BIND THE STONE TO THE WOOD** using twine or lengths of leather. Make sure you run the twine or leather around the piece of hardwood a few times just under the axe head, to discourage more splitting.

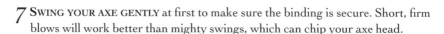
(5)

6 **FIND A PIECE OF WOOD** nobody wants and try your new axe out!

7 **SWING YOUR AXE GENTLY** at first to make sure the binding is secure. Short, firm blows will work better than mighty swings, which can chip your axe head.

DID YOU KNOW? You can also use flints to start a fire. If you strike a piece of steel against a flint stone, or run a piece of flint along a steel blade, it will produce sparks. In the olden days, these were directed onto dry tinder to light a fire. You can try it for yourself, but be very careful not to set fire to dry grass or brush that can cause a wildfire.

A radio

✦✦✦

If you're looking for a project that will impress and entertain your friends, make your own radio. This radio will be small enough to fit into a backpack during outdoor adventures and it doesn't need electricity or batteries to work. Actual radio signals travel at the speed of light and pass right through humans, buildings and other objects. All you have to do is pick up the signals.

Our project is what's known as a crystal radio. The electric energy in the radio waves actually powers the device so it doesn't need batteries. Early experimenters used a crystal rock inside the device to pick up stations – that's why they were called crystal radios. Now though, we can use a diode which makes it easier to pick up signals. These home-made radios were often constructed by Allied prisoners of war stuck in camps during World War II, so they could hear the latest news of the war's progress in spite of their captors.

DID YOU KNOW? Radios were first invented in various incarnations in the 1880s by several men. Nikola Tesla is credited in the United States with being the inventor of the radio, but Guglielmo Marconi received the Nobel Prize for Physics in 1909 for his work on 'wireless telegraphy', which was what people used to call radio transmission.

This is a challenging project that you'll need to get some help with. Together, you and a friend can put it together in an hour, once you know what you're doing. There are five basic components to a crystal radio: an antenna (and ground wire), a coil, a tuning capacitor, a detector and a headphone. Most of the supplies sound complicated but they are easy to find at a local electrical supply shop. The one part that's difficult to find is the headphone. You can't use regular ones; they have to be 1,000 ohm 'crystal' or 'impedance' earpieces. A shop selling electronics may sell them. If they don't, they might have catalogues that you can use to order one. If you get really stuck, you can buy kits containing all the components.

YOU WILL NEED

- A cylinder roughly 8 cm (3 in) long and 4 cm (1½ in) in diameter. Plastic, wood or paper will work – don't use metal
- 9 m (30 ft) of 24-gauge insulated hookup wire for the coil
- A long piece of wire with an alligator clip attached to one end (this is the antenna)
- Black electrical tape
- A diode
- A capacitor
- A headphone

STEPS

1 **MAKE THE COIL** by wrapping the insulated wire around a cylinder. Do not overlap the coils. Let the end of the wire extend off the cylinder by at least 12 cm (5 in). This is the grounding wire – you need to attach this end to a water pipe or some other metal rod that extends into the earth whenever you want to use the radio.

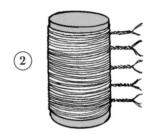

2 **AFTER SIX TURNS,** cut the wire and strip off 2.5 cm (1 in) of insulation. Then strip off 2.5 cm (1 in) of insulation from the other side of the cut wire and twist the two exposed ends together. Continue wrapping. You should have a point on the coil where a section of naked metal wire sticks up.

3 **AFTER 10 TURNS,** strip insulation and twist again. Keep doing this every 10 turns. Stop wrapping when you get to 65 turns. Extend the end of the coil wire 12 cm (5 in) off the cylinder and cut. Twist this wire onto the right fork of your capacitor.

4 **TWIST ONE END** of the diode onto the right fork of the capacitor. Check which end of the diode is which, since the radio will not work if it's the wrong way up.

5 **CUT A 15 CM (6-IN) LENGTH** of wire and strip off an inch of insulation from each end. Twist one end of this wire onto the twisted wires at turn six on your coil and twist its other end to the left fork of the capacitor.

6 THE CRYSTAL EARPIECE will have two wire ends. Attach one to the free end of the diode and another to the left fork of the capacitor.

7 USE BLACK ELECTRICAL TAPE to tape down the wires twisted onto the ends of the capacitor, and the twisted connection between the diode and the earpiece wire.

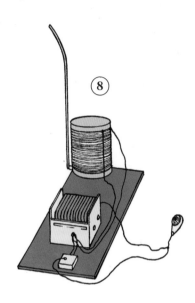

8 CLIP THE BLACK ALLIGATOR ANTENNA wire onto any of the twisted coil wires sticking out from the cylinder. You will use this to 'tune' the radio and can look for various stations by clipping and unclipping the alligator clip onto any of the wires sticking out from the coil.

9 ONCE THE ALL WIRES ARE ATTACHED you should be able to hear music in the earpiece straight away.

WARNING

Don't use your crystal radio during a thunderstorm. Make sure the antenna is grounded.

Eavesdropping on aircraft

❧❧

You're in your treehouse and enemy bombers are close at hand. You must break their secret code and inform your group of their location. Here's how to listen in on close-flying aircraft.

YOU WILL NEED

● A short-wave radio set

A short-wave radio is a set that picks up radio signals that have shorter frequencies than those we receive through common car or home radios.

Short frequency waves travel farther than normal ones, making them good for long-distance broadcasts as well as emergency communication. Ships and aeroplanes commonly use short-wave radio frequencies, which means you can pick up on their communications if you have a short-wave radio set.

The number of hertz describes the frequency of a radio signal. 'Mega' means one million, so one megahertz (MHz) is a million hertz. When aeroplane pilots send radio communications they do it at frequencies between 3 MHz and 30 MHz. Some signals are broadcast in kilohertz (kHz) instead of MHz – 'kilo' means a thousand, so one MHz is a thousand kHz (a thousand thousands is a million). If you have a wave that is at 9,000 kHz, then you can divide this number by 1,000 to express it in MHz, so 9,000 / 1,000 = 9 MHz.

To spy on nearby aeroplane communications you need to use the dial or digital tuner on your short-wave radio to search through the frequencies displayed on the radio band. Turn it very slowly. The best frequencies to try are:

4,650 – 4,750 kHz
6,545 – 6,765 kHz
8,815 – 9,040 kHz
11,175 – 11,400 kHz
13,200 – 13,360 kHz
15,010 – 15,100 kHz
17,900 – 18,030 kHz

A pinhole camera

The first type of camera ever invented was called a *camera obscura*, which is Latin for 'dark room'. At first, that's exactly what it was – a large, dark room with a tiny hole in one wall that allowed a narrow beam of light to enter. Many Renaissance painters would use these dark rooms and small light-holes to project images onto canvases, which they would trace to make more realistic paintings.

Your camera doesn't have to be anywhere near this big. In fact, this camera will be small enough to capture your next adventure on film. A camera works by exposing film to light. Chemicals on the film react to the light and create an image of whatever is in front of the film when the light reaches it. To create an image, the light needs to be focused. Modern cameras use a lens to focus light onto the film, but before these were commonly used, people relied on pinhole cameras. These are essentially light-proof boxes with a hole the size of a pin in the front. Because the pinhole is so small, it creates a focused image on the film inside the box.

Making the camera

The hardest part about making a pinhole camera is making sure no extra light gets in to spoil your photo. The secret is to ensure that black felt covers all the gaps.

YOU WILL NEED

- A small shoebox
- A craft knife
- Tin foil
- Self-adhesive black felt paper
- Masking tape
- A needle
- Two small paperclips
- Black insulating tape
- 7.5- x 12.5-cm (3- x 5-in) photo paper
- Two wide elastic bands large enough to fit around the box

STEPS

1 USE A CRAFT KNIFE to cut 2.5-cm (1 in) square hole in the middle of the bottom of a shoebox.

2 CUT A 5-CM (2-IN) SQUARE piece of tin foil and tape it to the inside of the shoebox so that it completely covers the square hole you just cut.

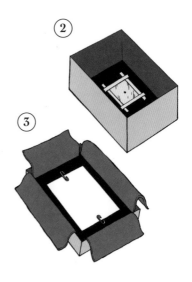

3 IN THE MIDDLE OF THE INSIDE of the lid just opposite the tin foil, create a film holder. Since we'll be using ch 7.5- x 12.5-cm (3- x 5-in) pieces of photo paper, use two small paper clips spaced no more than 12.5 cm (5 in) apart – one to hold the top of the paper and one to hold the bottom – and tape them securely in place.

4 COVER THE INSIDES OF THE BOX, including the inside of the lid, with self-adhesive black felt paper. Make sure the felt overlaps itself at the corners. Do not cover the piece of tin foil – just overlap its edges by 1 cm (½ in). Cover the area around the paper clips on the inside of the lid as much as possible, and let the black felt extend down the sides of the lid so that when the lid goes onto the box there will be a light-proof seal all the way around.

5 CREATE THE PINHOLE by making a tiny hole in the middle of the tin foil with a pin. For this size camera the pinhole should be roughly 0.5 mm in diameter.

6 MAKE THE CAMERA 'SHUTTER' by taping a thick piece of paper or cardboard over the pinhole. Just tape one side so that the paper can hinge open and closed. Put a piece of tape on the unhinged side so that you'll be able to keep the shutter closed when there's photo paper inside the camera.

7 COVER THE OUTSIDE OF THE BOX in black tape to further keep light out. At this point you can also put your name or other decorations on the outside with coloured tape.

HOW TO TAKE A PICTURE WITH A PINHOLE CAMERA

1 GO TO A COMPLETELY DARK PLACE and clip a piece of photo paper in place on the inside of the shoebox lid.

2 PUT THE LID ON THE BOX and secure it in place using two elastic bands at the top and bottom of the lid.

3 PLACE THE CAMERA ON A STABLE SURFACE opposite your photography subject.

4 WHEN YOU'RE READY TO TAKE THE PICTURE, open the shutter for about 20 seconds in bright light, 40 seconds in partly cloudy light, and about four minutes in low light. You'll have to do some experimentation to see what length of time works best.

5 CLOSE THE SHUTTER.

6 TO DEVELOP THE PHOTO PAPER you can take it to a photo shop – make sure you don't expose the photo paper to any more light on the way.

7 THOSE WHO WANT TO DEVELOP AT HOME need to have four paper trays filled with developer solution, stop solution, fix solution and water. Your local camera store can fix you up and give you instructions on using them.

The camera works by only letting a very small amount of light through the pinhole, which focuses it on the light-sensitive paper to take the picture. When light comes through the pinhole in your camera it inverts the image you're taking so that it ends up upside down on the paper.

DID YOU KNOW? Modern cameras use lenses to focus the light, which gives them a much clearer picture of a more distinct area. Today they also use digital light sensors to record images as computer files, instead of directly onto film or paper.

A kite

❖

Reach up to the skies with a home-made kite. This can be quite fiddly, so an extra pair of hands is probably a good idea. With a bit of help you can build a great kite in about 45 minutes.

DID YOU KNOW? The Chinese invented kites thousands of years ago to use during wartime. Soldiers would attach fireworks to them and fly them up over the enemy, where they would explode and frighten off invading troops. Or they would use kites to carry explosives over distances that cannons couldn't reach. Kites of different colours were also used to relay messages, since they could be seen over very long distances.

YOU WILL NEED

- One straight, thin piece of cane about 90 cm (3 ft) long
- One straight, thin piece of cane 45 cm (18 in) long
- A good length of thick twine
- A long kite string
- Scissors
- A large piece of thick white paper, at least 90 x 30 cm (3 x 1 ft)
- Masking tape
- Ribbon

STEPS

1 CUT THIN, SHALLOW NOTCHES in the ends of both lengths of cane. These notches don't have to be thicker than the blade of the knife.

2 MAKE A CROSS by placing the shorter piece of cane over the longer piece. They should intersect about a foot down on the longer piece.

3 SECURE THEM IN PLACE by lashing them with thick twine. Pass the twine round the crossing point in an 'X', and tuck the end under the loops to finish off.

4 NOW MAKE A TIGHT FRAME OF TWINE around the canes, using the notches you made in step 1 as guides. First make a loop in the end of the twine, using a bowline knot (see page 13). Lodge the knot on one notch (so the loop hangs free the other side) and stretch the string all the way around, passing through each notch until you come back to the loop.

5 PASS THE TWINE THROUGH THE LOOP and stretch it back round the frame in the reverse direction. Repeat steps 4 and 5 a few times. This will make the twine frame taut. Be careful not to make it too tight or the canes will warp.

6 LAY THE CANE and twine frame over your sheet of paper. Trace around the kite frame onto the paper, giving yourself at least 2.5 cm (1 in) extra paper all around the outline.

7 CUT THE SHAPE OF THE KITE out of the paper. Don't forget to make the paper a little larger than the kite. Attach the paper to the face of the cane kite frame by folding the extra width of paper over the twine all the way around, and taping it to the back.

8 CREATE THE KITE 'HARNESS' by tying a piece of twine at the top and bottom of the long piece of cane, and another piece at the ends of the shorter piece of cane. They should intersect about 15 cm (6 in) above the intersection of the canes. Tie the two pieces of twine together at that point, and make a small twine loop in one of the tied ends. This is where you'll attach your kite string when you're ready to fly.

9 MAKE A KITE TAIL with a 90-cm (3-ft) length of twine. Tie 10-cm (4-in) pieces of ribbon to the twine every 15 cm (6 in) or so as decoration.

10 TIE THE KITE STRING TO THE LOOP, and you're ready to take your kite outside on a windy day and launch!

You can fly your kite as is, or you can colour or paint it however you like. Make sure your decoration is even so that your kite stays balanced – if you have too much weight on one side, the kite will spin out of control when the wind blows and crash rather than fly.

A wooden whistle

✦ ✦

If you're ever camping, a whistle can come in very handy for attracting attention, especially if you get lost. Knowing how to whittle a piece of wood into a whistle can come in handy, too, especially if you've got some time to kill on a family holiday miles away from your backyard.

This project is moderately challenging. You'll need to find the wood and drill a hole in the end of it before you go. A straight piece of cherry wood about 7.5 cm (3 in) long with a diameter of about 1.3 cm (½ in) should do the trick. Wooden dowels bought at the hardware store work well. Drill into one end about 6 cm (2½ in) deep and 0.5 cm (¼-in) wide. Once the hole is drilled, you can pack the wood and other supplies along with you and whittle the rest in camp. It will take several hours to complete.

YOU WILL NEED ⚠

- Pre-drilled 7.5-cm (3-in) length of wood
- A small dowel 2.5-cm (1-in) long and 0.5 cm (¼-in) wide

- A saw
- A sharp knife
- Sandpaper
- Wood glue

STEPS

1 USE THE SAW TO CUT A NOTCH in the drilled end of the stick of larger dowel to create a hole in the top of the wood. The notch will reveal the long drilled hole at the centre of the wood. It should be about 9-mm (⅜-in) deep and 12 mm (½-in) long.

2 SAND THE LENGTH OF ONE SIDE of the wooden dowel so that you end up with a semi-circular dowel with one side flat.

3 SLIDE THE DOWEL into the pre-drilled hole at the end of the whistle, flat side up. Don't push it all the way in. It should stop just before it reaches the notch cut in the top of the whistle.

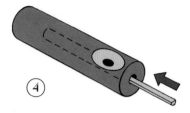

4 BLOW ON THE END OF THE WHISTLE to test the pitch and pull or push the dowel in or out to get the sound you want. Getting a sound should be relatively easy. You shouldn't have to turn red in the face from blowing, nor should the sound have a lot of air to it. If you can't get a note, try another piece of dowel with less wood sanded off it.

5 ONCE YOU GET THE SOUND YOU WANT, hold the dowel in place and cut it flush with the end of the whistle.

6 REMOVE THE DOWEL, put a thin bead of wood glue on its rounded side and push it back in. Leave it for a few minutes to set.

7 USE A WHITTLING KNIFE to shape the whistle. Box off the end that you blow on and make it smaller, or carve decorations into the side.

A whistle like this works just the same way as when you whistle with your mouth. Air passing through the hole under pressure starts to vibrate. When the speed of the air, and the shape and size of the hole are correct, the vibrations resonate to make sound.

Whistles can be very useful on adventures: the loud noise can scare off wild animals or attract attention if you're lost and need help. You can even use one to signal SOS (see page 21). Or you can just take it along to keep the players in order next time you're referee for a football match.

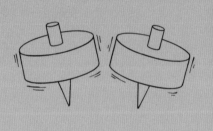

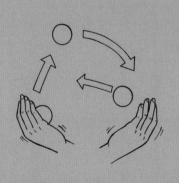

Chapter Five

Fun!

ADVENTURE CAN BE A SERIOUS PASTIME
but let's not forget that, in the end, we're in this
for some fun! If you're getting frustrated building
a radio, or your pinhole-camera photos aren't
coming out the way you'd like them to, try
learning a few of these games and tricks.

✦

Plus, a well-fought game of conkers or
draughts is a great way to feed those competitive
impulses. Can't beat an older brother at football
or wrestling? Show him who's boss on
the game board.

Spinning tops

— ❖ ❖ —

Another easy project to make is a spinning top. What's fun about these is the decoration and shape of the top, and what it looks like while it's spinning. Or if you're in a more competitive mood you can make fighting tops and have competitions with your friends. You can make your tops square, round, or triangular. Try painting them in different colours or patterns. Spirals on round tops can play tricks on the eyes once they get going.

Making a decorative top

YOU WILL NEED
- Thick cardboard
- Wooden skewers
- Scissors
- Glue or tape

STEPS

1 CUT THE SHAPE OF YOUR TOP or tops out of the cardboard. You can make them any shape you like, but remember, if it's too heavy on one side it might not spin evenly.

2 DECORATE THE TOP with bright colours and patterns. Try different patterns and see what effect is produced when you spin them.

3 PUSH A WOODEN SKEWER through the centre of the top. Leave most of the skewer above the cardboard, and just a short amount below it where the sharp tip of the skewer touches the ground. Glue or tape the skewer to secure it in place.

4 TO SPIN THE TOP, use your fingers and give it a quick twist, by rolling the skewer between your thumb and middle finger as if you were snapping.

Making a fighting top

You might find cardboard tops a bit lightweight for fighting, so experiment with tops made out of cork, wooden dowel or plastic. You could even whittle your own using the same techniques as for making a whistle (see page 122). Try different designs with different materials and see if you can build a winner. Here's one way to do it.

YOU WILL NEED

- A 2-cm (1-in) length of 2-cm- (1-in-) thick dowel
- A drill with a 5-mm (¼-inch) bit
- A 4-cm (2-in) length of 5-mm- (¼-in-) thick dowel
- Wood glue
- A knife

STEPS

1 DRILL A HOLE 5 mm (¼ in) across, right down the centre of your thick piece of dowel, so you're left with a wooden ring. This will be the body of your top.

2 USE YOUR KNIFE to trim the short end of the thin dowel to a point, so your top can spin on it. (Or you can use an ordinary pencil-sharpener to make the point, if you want a shortcut.)

3 PUT A DAB OF GLUE on the end of a matchstick and smear it inside the hole in the thick dowel.

4 PUSH THE LENGTH OF NARROW DOWEL into the hole so it sticks out about 5 mm (¼ in) on the other side. Quickly wipe off any glue on the protruding end before it dries.

5 WHEN THE GLUE DRIES, paint your top, or use your knife to carve designs on it and streamline its shape however you want. Make a couple of tops yourself, or encourage your friends to make their own, so you can challenge them.

Top fights

YOU WILL NEED

- 2 tops
- A friend to compete with
- Chalk or something else to mark out a ring
- Flat ground

STEPS

1 **WITH YOUR CHALK OR A STICK,** mark out a circle about 30 cm (1 ft) in diameter on a piece of flat ground.

2 **YOU AND A FRIEND TAKE A TOP EACH** and set them spinning as fast as you can in the ring. Then steer them into each other by blowing on them. When they collide, they'll go spinning off in different directions.

3 **THE WINNER** is the top that knocks the other one over, or pushes it out of the ring, but keeps on spinning itself.

DID YOU KNOW? Fighting tops are very popular all across Asia, where a wok (a large, round-bottomed pan) is often used instead of a ring. The curved sides keep the tops together so their owners don't need to blow them together. Some fighting tops have gyroscopes – mechanisms built in to make them harder to knock over, keeping the fights going for longer.

Performing magic tricks

❖

Magic has always had a special appeal for boys of all ages.
Learning some sleight of hand is a bit like running away with
the circus – except you don't have to leave home. Coin and card
tricks are the best magic for beginners. Learn a few of these
tricks, and you'll be vanishing elephants on stage before you
can say hocus pocus.

Harry Houdini wasn't always an escape artist. He actually started out in the late
1900s doing card tricks and other magic performances. His tombstone in
Machpelah Cemetery in Queens, New York, is decorated with the crest of the
Society of American Magicians.

Magical disappearing coin trick

YOU WILL NEED
- 2 coins
- 2 hands
- Practice

STEPS

1 PLACE A COIN in each hand, palms up, above a table. Place the coin in your left
hand in the middle of your palm, but place the coin in your right palm closer to
your thumb.

2 FLIP YOUR HANDS OVER QUICKLY and slam them onto the table. The coin in
your right hand, because of its location in your palm, should fly off your right
palm and under your left palm.

3 SLOWLY LIFT YOUR RIGHT HAND to show that the coin in that hand has
disappeared . . . and magically moved to your left hand (show both coins under
your left hand now).

The amazing mistaken card trick

YOU WILL NEED

- Cards
- Basic counting ability

STEPS

1 BEFORE YOU BEGIN, secretly place a card of your choosing (let's say it's the ace of hearts) seven places from the top of the deck.

2 AFTER SELECTING A MEMBER of the audience to help, declare that you will force the audience member to pick your favourite card – in this case, the ace of hearts.

3 ASK THE AUDIENCE MEMBER to pick a number between 10 and 30. That is the number of cards you will pull off the top of the deck to reveal the ace of hearts.

4 BEGIN COUNTING, placing each card face down on top of the one before it, but don't stop at the number the audience member selected. Instead, count past it by exactly seven cards – so if they pick 12, count off 19 cards. At that point, pretend you're confused and declare that you've gone past their number.

5 PLACE THE ALREADY-COUNTED CARDS on top of the deck and hand it to the volunteer. Then ask them to count – say that it's more fair that way anyway.

6 WHEN THEY PEEL OFF CARDS equal to the number they selected, they'll reach the ace of hearts. Abracadabra!

The real trick for any magic is to be confident. The more you look like you know what you're doing, the easier it is to persuade your audience to believe in your illusion. Professional magicians practise a running speech during their tricks, called a 'patter', that makes their actions appear natural, and distracts the audience at the key moment.

WARNING

Never show anybody the same trick more than once! The more times they see it, the greater the chance they'll work out how it's done. A true magician never reveals his secrets.

Playing the drums

❧ ❧

The key to playing the drums like a pro is knowing how to hold the drumsticks. Our instinct is to hold them like grilled chicken legs and pound away, but you get much more control by cradling the sticks in your hands so that the end is in the crook between your thumb and index finger and the mid-point is being held by the tips of the fingers. Then it's all about keeping the beat.

YOU WILL NEED

- A drum kit
- Drumsticks
- Rhythm

STEPS

1 SIT DOWN AT A DRUM KIT and position your hands and feet right. First, place one foot above the bass drum pedal. Put your toe on the pedal and keep your heel raised. This allows you to move your foot more quickly when hitting the bass drum.

2 THE RIGHT HAND will cross the left to play the hi-hat cymbals while the left plays the snare drum directly in front of you.

3 DRUMMERS TYPICALLY KEEP TIME by tapping the hi-hat. To keep a 4/4 beat going – the most common beat for rock and pop songs – hit the hi-hat four times per bar (on every beat) and the bass drum and snare every other beat.

4 AFTER SOME PRACTICE you should be able to mix in a few flourishes as you develop your own personal drumming style.

Winning at draughts

❖ ❖

Draughts is one of the all-time great games. It's also one of the oldest. The board game may have been played as far back as 1400 B.C., and Plato made reference to it in Ancient Greece in the fourth and fifth centuries B.C. In eighteenth-century America, the name 'checkers' was adopted for the game, whereas in France it is known as 'dames'.

Today, there's no better game to pack along on a family holiday for quick and easy playtime. Anyone can play, and learn to play well – all it takes is a few practice rounds.

DID YOU KNOW? There are at least nine different ways to play checkers, and many countries have their own distinct rules. In Canada, for example, players play on a 12x12 square board with 30 pieces each while in Poland, players use a 10x10 square board with 20 pieces on each side. The most common rules are the ones for English draughts or American checkers.

YOU WILL NEED
- An 8 x 8 square chess board
- 12 black and 12 white draughts pieces
- 2 players

HOW TO PLAY

1 EACH PLAYER sets up three rows of pieces across the board, using the dark squares only.

2 BLACK GETS TO MOVE FIRST. Toss a coin to decide who gets to play black and who plays white.

3 THE AIM IS TO CAPTURE all the opposing player's pieces, or force the other player into a position in which he cannot move. Whoever captures all the other player's pieces first wins.

4 PLAYERS CAN ONLY MOVE diagonally into an unoccupied square. You can only move one square at a time on a normal move, but more if you capture. If a player cannot move any of his or her pieces, he loses the game.

5 TO CAPTURE AN OPPONENT'S PIECE, a player jumps diagonally over it with one of their pieces, landing in the square beyond. It's only possible to jump over one of the opposing player's pieces if the square on the other side is vacant. A piece can jump over more than one opposing piece in one move, as long as there's a space in between each piece it captures. You have to 'leapfrog' over each piece to capture it.

6 IT'S AGAINST THE RULES to pass up a jump in favour of a normal diagonal move. That goes for multiple jumps, too. If you have the opportunity to jump multiple times you must do it.

7 IF YOU ARE ABLE to get a piece into the last row (or the opposing player's first row, also known as the 'king's row') that piece is 'kinged' or 'crowned'. The most common way to indicate this is to put a captured piece underneath the crowned piece, so it stands above the rest of the board. The player's turn ends when a piece moves into king's row and is crowned. A crowned piece can move forwards and backwards, which makes having one a big advantage!

The rules are very simple, but as you'll soon see, the game can quickly get complicated. Some good tactics to remember are:

Always watch out for double or triple captures, which can win the game for you, or let your opponent cut your army in half if you're not careful. Remember that kings can capture forwards *and* backwards, which can really mess up your plans if you're not expecting it.

Your pieces cannot be captured if they're in a square on the edge of the board, because there's nowhere on the other side for enemy pieces to jump to. This can be a useful defence early in the game.

Later in the game, pieces on the edges of the board can get trapped, because the number of squares they can move to is smaller. This can force you into a bad position where you have to let some of your pieces get captured, so be careful.

Playing marbles

❧

Contrary to what most kids might think, marbles isn't just a boring game your grandfather used to play while he waited for video games to be invented. It actually takes skill and strategy to win. And it gives you something to do when you're adventuring in the great outdoors far from the nearest plug or battery charger.

DID YOU KNOW? Marbles really is an old game. There are references to the game in Roman literature from over 2,000 years ago.

YOU WILL NEED

- 2 players
- 13 small marbles
- 2 big marbles, called the 'shooters'
- A flat, open patch of dirt at least 3 m (10 ft) around

HOW TO PLAY

1 USE A STICK to draw a 3-m- (10-ft-) diameter circle in the dirt. This is going to be your playing area, so make sure it's good and clear.

2 TO DECIDE WHO GOES FIRST, each player stands on one edge of the circle and tries to flick his or her shooter as close as possible to the opposite side of the circle without going outside the line. The player whose marble lands closest to the line without crossing it, wins the first shot.

3 ONCE YOU'VE DETERMINED who shoots first, place the 13 smaller marbles in a cross pattern in the middle of the circle.

4 THE FIRST PLAYER STANDS OUTSIDE THE CIRCLE and flicks his shooter at the marbles. To flick the marble, use the tip of your thumb with the shooter resting

on the side of your index finger. Your knuckles should be aimed at the ground but they cannot touch the ground. The goal of the game is to knock the smaller marbles out of the circle.

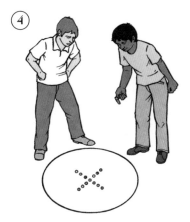

5 WHEN A PLAYER KNOCKS OUT A SMALLER MARBLE he can take another turn, and continue shooting until he fails to knock a smaller marble out. After the first turn, you shoot from wherever your shooter landed inside the circle on the last shot. Any marbles you knock out of the ring, keep to one side in your own pile – this is how you keep score.

6 IF YOU FAIL TO KNOCK A MARBLE OUT, your opponent takes over and you cannot move your shooter from where it sits in the ring until he finishes his turn (by failing to knock any marbles out with one of his throws).

7 NOW YOUR OPPONENT HAS TWO OPTIONS. He can a) try to knock out the small marbles or b) try to knock your shooter out of the ring. If they succeed in knocking out your shooter, then they get to keep all the marbles you've gathered, and you lose the game.

8 YOU CAN WIN by either knocking your opponent's shooter out of the ring, or by having more marbles than your opponent when all the small ones have been knocked out.

DID YOU KNOW? There are many other variations of the game, with different layouts of marbles in the ring; opposing 'armies' of marbles, where each player has to knock out his opponent's men while keeping his own men safe; and even a 'golf' version popular in Taiwan, where each player has to flick his marble into a series of holes. Half the fun can be making up your own rules, so be creative!

Playing conkers

❖

If you enjoy the crack of two marbles bashing into each other and the joy of watching your opponent's pieces sail out of the circle, you're going to love conkers. Conkers is a game based on tying a large nut from the horse-chestnut tree to a piece of string, and bashing it into someone else's conker until one of them breaks.

The game of conkers started in England in the nineteenth century and is sometimes referred to as 'conquerors', since one person's conker is indeed trying to conquer another's. Other names for the game include 'obblyonkers', 'cheggies' or 'cheesers'. Every year there is a World Conkers Championship held in England, where conker competitors from around the world come to compete. The winner is crowned with, you guessed it, more conkers.

Making the conker

To make a proper gaming conker, you'll need an electric drill.

YOU WILL NEED
- A large horse chestnut
- An electric drill
- String or a shoelace

STEPS

1 CHOOSE THE BIGGEST HORSE CHESTNUT you can find and drill a hole through the centre of it.

2 PUT A LENGTH OF STRING about the length of a shoelace (a spare shoelace is perfect if you've got one) into the hole, and tie a fat knot at the end so the conker will stay securely on the string.

3 LET THE GAMES BEGIN.

To make sure the conker you're using is as strong as possible, drill a clean, straight hole and check there are no notches or cracks in the nut. Given that the aim of the game is to break the conker, you should probably make a few spares to take along to your tournament.

Playing the game

YOU WILL NEED

- Conkers on strings
- At least two players, but preferably more

STEPS

1 FLIP A COIN to determine who attacks first. The winner is the striker and the loser is the defender.

2 OPPOSING PLAYERS STAND NEXT TO EACH OTHER. The defender holds his conker out in front of him, with the string wrapped around two fingers.

3 THE STRIKER WRAPS THE END of his string around one index finger and holds the actual nut in his other hand. When he's ready, he tries to hit the defender's conker with his own as hard as he can. The defender is not allowed to move.

4 THE STRIKER IS GIVEN THREE TRIES. Once he scores a hit, the players switch roles. If he misses with all three swings, tough luck – they still swap over.

5 DURING A STRIKE, if the strings get tangled, whoever shouts 'Strings!' first wins the next strike.

6 IF A PLAYER DROPS HIS CONKER, then his opponent can shout 'Stamps!' and stamp on his conker, unless the player shouts 'No stamps!' first.

7 IF A PLAYER'S CONKER IS STRUCK by the striker and it spins in a full circle this is called 'Around the World' and the striker gets to go again.

8 THE GAME ENDS when one of the conkers is smashed off its string.

Diving into water

❖ ❖ ❖

Diving into a pool filled with cool, refreshing water during the height of summer is a great mix of fun and thrills, especially if the drop is more than 3 m (10 ft) above the surface. Some say it's a little like flying, unless of course you land flat on your back. Then the thrills give way to the reality of a burning sting of bright red, slapped skin.

How to make a big splash

Sometimes you want to make a show and send a stream of water high above the pool – or over the side and onto a group of sunbathing girls. The biggest splash of all comes from landing flat on your stomach ('belly flopping'), but this really hurts! Try it from any kind of height and it'll knock the breath out of you. Here's how to make a big splash without injuring yourself.

YOU WILL NEED

● Deep water ● Swimming trunks

STEPS

1 ONE WAY TO ENSURE AN EXPLOSION OF WATER straight up is to make a cannonball. While in the air, tuck your legs to your chest and hold them close with your feet. You want to enter the water at a slight angle so you don't smack the front of your legs on the surface. Hold your legs even after you hit the water to ensure the largest splash.

2 A WAY TO DIRECT YOUR SPLASH is to do a somersault dive. Stand on the side of the pool or on a diving board and dive in. As your head hits the water, tuck your chin down to your chest and roll forward as if you're doing a somersault. As your body rolls over, it will make a large splash in the direction you are diving.

How to make a small splash

There are also times you want to show off your stealth and knife through the water silently. This takes some practice.

YOU WILL NEED
- Deep water
- Swimming trunks

STEPS

1 START BY SITTING on the poolside with your legs dangling in the water. Brace your feet against the side of the pool, point your arms over your head, with your hands held tightly together, and use your legs to launch yourself into the pool.

2 WHEN YOU'RE COMFORTABLE with the sitting dive, you can graduate to crouching. Crouch on the side of the pool with your arms in the same position, and lean forward until you slip silently into the water.

3 WHEN YOU'RE CONFIDENT with both these exercises, you can move on to the real thing! Stand on the side of the pool with your hands straight over your head and the insides of your elbows resting against your ears. Sometimes it helps to put your palms together.

4 JUMP UP AS HIGH as you can and bend your body in the air, then straighten it like a jackknife, so you come into the water as vertically as possible. If it's hard to come down

perfectly vertical, try to angle inwards rather than turning too far and falling over backwards, which will cause a splash every time.

5 AS YOU'RE ABOUT TO enter the water tighten your body muscles, especially your legs. Try to keep your feet together and point your toes.

6 ONCE YOU GET INTO THE WATER, move your hands and arms immediately in a swimming motion back towards your sides. This will prevent a large splash, and instead cause the surface of the water to foam as the air bubbles rise from your entry.

> **WARNING**
>
> Always check how deep the water is before diving, and always check carefully for shallow rocks or other objects on or near the surface.

As you get more confident and your skills increase, you can start using diving boards. It's a great feeling to fly through the air and still hit the water with barely a splash! Start with the lower ones so you get used to the increased impact of hitting the water from higher up. A lifeguard at your local pool will likely be able to show you where to start.

Trained competition divers jump from as high as 10 m (30 ft), and can perform all sorts of mid-air manoeuvres as they fall. Diving competitions are held as part of the Olympic games, where each dive is given marks out of ten by expert judges based on a smooth take-off, impressive mid-air gymnastics, and the least splashy entry into the water.

DID YOU KNOW? In Acapulco, Mexico, specially trained athletes dive off cliffs 34 m (110 ft) high into seawater only about 4 m (13 ft) deep. They have to time their jumps to coincide with incoming waves, or the water will be too shallow and they will injure themselves on the rocky sea bed. These divers enter the water at 90 kmph (55 mph). The impact is so forceful that, to prevent broken hands, fingers, and noses, they have to go in head- rather than face-first and clench their fists above their heads.

Wolf-whistling

If you foresee a future in building construction, or you're planning to hail a few cabs in New York City, you'll need to learn this one. And anyway, it's good fun to know how to whistle and whistle loud – which is what you get when you use your fingers and your mouth for the wolf whistle. You never know when you'll need to make noise for the home side.

YOU WILL NEED
- Your mouth
- Your lips
- Your tongue
- Two clean fingers

STEPS

1 TUCK YOUR LIPS INWARDS so they cover your teeth and are tucked back into your mouth.

2 PLACE TWO FINGERS of your choice between the corners and centre of your mouth (you can use the thumb and middle finger of either hand, your right and left index fingers, or your right and left pinkie fingers). They should be one knuckle into your mouth.

3 ANGLE YOUR FINGERNAILS INWARDS towards the centre of your tongue and make your lips firm.

4 ANGLE THE TONGUE by drawing it back so that the front touches the bottom of your mouth a short distance from your gums.

5 BLOW.

Juggling

✦✦✦

Juggling is lots of fun and a great way to impress your friends, and it can keep you entertained for hours. Master this simple method, and next thing you know you'll be auditioning for the circus.

DID YOU KNOW? During the Middle Ages, jugglers were known as 'gleemen' and were thought to have loose morals. Some were even accused of witchcraft!

Juggling is difficult to start, so build up in stages. Here are some exercises to get you going. One good tip is to start by throwing the balls higher than you normally would, to get an idea of what the pattern is like.

YOU WILL NEED
- 3 round, light objects of equal size, or professionally made juggling balls

BEGINNER

1 HOLD TWO BALLS in your right hand and one in your left. Throw one ball from your right hand and catch it in the left.

2 THROW THE BALL BACK from your left hand and catch it in your right. Easy so far, right?

3 PRACTISE until you never drop any of the balls. When you're feeling confident, move onto the next stage.

INTERMEDIATE

1 AGAIN, START WITH TWO BALLS held in your right hand and one ball held in your left.

2 THROW ONE BALL FROM YOUR RIGHT HAND as you did for the beginner's practice. As it reaches the top of its arc, throw the ball in your left hand.

3 CATCH THE FIRST BALL YOU THREW in your left hand, and the second ball you threw in your right hand. The two balls should have exchanged places.

4 AGAIN, PRACTISE THIS until you can do it without ever dropping a ball.

ADVANCED

1 PUT TWO BALLS in your right hand and one in your left.

2 START BY THROWING ONE of the balls in your right hand up and slightly to the left.

3 THEN THROW THE BALL in your left hand up and under the ball you just threw, as you did in the intermediate practice.

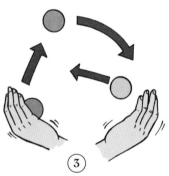

4 AS YOU CATCH THE FIRST BALL in your left hand throw the last ball in the air and catch the second ball with your right hand.

5 YOU ARE ESSENTIALLY PLAYING CATCH with all three balls at the same time, so there's always a third ball in the air.

6 THIS CAN BE PRETTY DIFFICULT to start with, so keep practising – count the number of throws you can manage before dropping any of the balls, to see how well you're doing. Gradually build up speed as you gain more control, and soon you'll be juggling like a professional.

Throwing a boomerang

❖ ❖

Boomerangs were invented by the indigenous Australian people, who used them to hunt small game and birds. They would throw them in the hope of whacking the animal on the head; if they missed, the tool would circle back around in the air so the hunter would catch it and try again.

YOU WILL NEED

- A small-ish boomerang
- Large open space

STEPS

1 HOLD THE BOOMERANG in between your thumb and the side of your index finger on the tip of one wing. The flat end should be facing outwards and the boomerang should be almost vertical, with a slight tilt outwards, and the free wing pointing forwards.

2 IT'S NOT IMPORTANT TO THROW THE BOOMERANG HARD. Simply hold it back just behind your ear and flip it forward with some force. More important is to get lots of spin into the throw. Use your wrist to get as much spin as possible.

3 THE BOOMERANG SHOULD LEVEL OFF on its own and curve in the air. If you throw it correctly, it should be possible to catch it between your hands as it curves back round.

4 THERE ARE LEFT- and right-handed boomerangs – make sure you get the right one. Left-handed boomerangs will curve one way and right-handed ones will curve the other.

WARNING

Don't throw a boomerang level like a Frisbee – it'll just fly straight up before crashing down in a pile of splinters.

Bowling a leg-spinner

❖❖

Spin-bowling – the art of getting a cricket ball to zigzag in unexpected directions after hitting the wicket – is one of the most useful cricket skills, and one of the hardest to master. A skilled spinner can unsettle any batsman, and either restrict their score or trick them into getting out. If you've ever fancied being the next Shane Warne or Monty Panesar, here are a few tips to get you started.

YOU WILL NEED
- A cricket ball
- A wicket to bowl on
- Stumps to bowl at

STEPS

1 START BY HOLDING THE BALL around the seam. Use the tips of your index and middle fingers to grip it, and rest your thumb and third finger along the seam.

2 SPIN-BOWLERS TEND TO BOWL fairly slowly, since it's the direction of the ball not its speed that deceives the batsman. This means you only need to run up a few paces before releasing the ball.

3 AS YOU RUN, hold the ball close to your chest. In the last stride of your run, straighten your arm, swinging it around above your head, and release the ball towards the stumps.

4 AS YOU RELEASE THE BALL, flip your wrist clockwise so the ball spins out of your hands. Flick your third finger along the seam to add extra spin in the same direction. The ball should land on the seam in front of the stumps and spin off to one side.

Skimming stones

+ +

For boys and their dads, there's a simple joy in picking up rocks and throwing them. It's been that way for generations before us and will be that way for generations to come. We like to throw them at trees, signs, cans – you name it. We've all been in trouble for it one time or another but we still throw them – just preferably not at anything breakable, like windows or other people.

One variation on the theme of stone-throwing is skimming stones. By throwing a flat stone in the right way, it's possible to make it bounce over the surface of a pond, lake, or river. Rare is the boy who comes across a body of water and doesn't throw something into it – stick, rock or leaf. This is just a way to introduce some skill into the equation. When you get older – like, say, your dad's age – skimming stones can be a great way to relax.

The key to skimming stones is the stone itself. The ideal skimming stone is a flat, oblong-shaped one with round edges. Perfectly round ones are good, but oblong ones give you a place to put your index finger to ensure the right spin. Combing the beach to find a good skimming stone is half the fu

---

DID YOU KNOW? Stone-skimming has a long and honourable history. In Greek legend, Hercules, the strongest man alive, was challenged to a discus-throwing competition by a young upstart. Hercules agreed, and hurled his discus so far out to sea that it landed on a nearby island. The boy, however, threw his discus like a skimming stone, so it bounced on the surface of the water and skipped out past the island. Hercules was so amused that legend says the two became close friends. The principle of a spinning object skipping across the surface of the water was part of the design of bouncing bombs, used by British airmen to destroy hydroelectric dams in Germany during World War II. These 'dambusters' were dropped from aeroplanes onto the surface of the water behind the dam, with enough backspin to make them skip across the water and explode against the concrete.

YOU WILL NEED

- Water
- Flat, oblong-shaped rocks with round edges

STEPS

1 POSITION THE ROCK IN YOUR HAND so that your thumb is on top of the rock, your index finger is wrapped around the front edge, and your middle and ring fingers are stabilising it underneath.

2 STAND SIDEWAYS TO THE WATER and pull your arm back, keeping the flat side of the rock parallel to the water.

3 FLING THE ROCK WITH A SIDE-ARM MOTION. Bend your knees so you get low to the ground. You want the rock to hit the water at as low an angle as possible. Let the rock spin out of your hand and off the end of your index finger so that it spins horizontally, like a Frisbee landing on the water.

4 THE HARDER YOUR FIRST THROW IS, the more the stone will 'take off' after the first skip. This can be fun, but it can also limit any further skims. Practise to get the speed of throw just right so your stone skips several times.

WARNING

Never skim stones in an area where there are swimmers. Skimmed stones can sometimes move erratically, and nobody likes a stone in the head.

5 IF YOU'RE SKIMMING ROCKS WITH FRIENDS, try to see who can get the longest distance between skips. Then see who can get the most skips. The world record number of skips with a single stone is 40!

DID YOU KNOW? The old-fashioned English name for skimming stones is 'playing ducks and drakes'. Over time, the phrase came to mean messing around, so they obviously didn't see it as a sensible pastime.

Serving in tennis

❖❖❖

Tennis is a game of skill that takes loads of practice. The hardest thing to learn to do well is the serve. OK, so it takes some strength and coordination, but technique plays just as much of a role in perfecting a good one. Crack it and you'll be hard to beat – if you can ace your opponent on a regular basis (that is, serve so well they can't hit the ball back), you won't have to worry so much about practising your backhand.

Just to review, the goal when you're serving in tennis is to hit the ball overhand across the net diagonally into the opposite service box. The server must stand behind the baseline while serving: if a foot crosses onto or over the line during the serve, it's a foot fault and the serve doesn't count. You get two tries to hit the ball into the opposite box, so tennis players usually go all-out on their first serve and try to hit it as hard as they can. If you don't get the ball into the service box on either try, you lose a point.

Now on to the service technique.

YOU WILL NEED

- A tennis court
- Tennis balls and a racket

STEPS

1 **STAND BEHIND THE BASELINE** about midway between the out-of-bounds line and the centre line.

2 **PLACE THE LENGTH OF YOUR LEFT FOOT** parallel to the baseline and lean your weight on that foot, leaving your right foot trailing behind about half a leg's length away. Bend your knees.

3 LINE YOUR SHOULDERS UP with the direction you want the ball to go in.

4 POINT YOUR RACKET towards the net.

5 IN ONE MOTION, sweep your racket down and up in an arc behind you. At the same time, toss the tennis ball up in as straight a line as possible just in front of you.

6 AS THE BALL GOES UP, bend your elbow to bring your racket up and behind you, as if you're about to scratch the middle of your back with it. Keep your wrist straight and firm.

7 ONCE THE BALL REACHES ITS HIGHEST POINT, bring the racket forwards and hit the ball. Keep it soft at first until your technique improves. Don't sacrifice control for speed.

8 AS SOON AS YOU HIT THE BALL, fold your wrist downwards and follow all the way through with your racket.

9 DON'T RELAX! If you're playing with an opponent, he'll be trying to hit the ball right back at you. Stay on your toes after you serve so you're ready for his return shot.

DID YOU KNOW? American tennis player Andy Roddick holds the record for the fastest recorded professional tennis serve at 250 kmph (155 mph).

Tackling in football

Football is a non-contact sport, so any time you tackle someone you must be careful to go for the ball rather than the player. This requires more skill than you might think, so here are some tips on how to get the ball cleanly. It can still get a little rough, though, so tighten up those shinpads.

DID YOU KNOW? Football has been played in Europe since the Middle Ages, but some believe it was actually first invented in China.

YOU WILL NEED

- A football
- Someone to tackle

Block tackle

Block tackles are the ones that happen most often on the field. You use this one when your opponent is charging towards you with the ball, and you have to stop him. If you do it properly, you stay on your feet, your opponent hits the deck, and you get the ball. Just put the inside of your foot on the ball as your opponent tries to dribble past you. If you time it correctly, you'll stop the ball suddenly and your opponent will trip over it, or lose control.

Poke tackle

This is just what it sounds like: a way to poke the ball away from your opponent. You can use this to tackle somebody from the side. Use whichever foot is closest to the ball: just try to stick your toe in front of him at the right moment, to send the ball in the wrong direction and keep it away from your goal. Although you're not guaranteed possession of the ball doing this, you'll take it away from your opponent, and cause some disruption so that hopefully a nearby teammate will come away with the ball.

Slide tackle

This is usually done when you're chasing the ball and the opponent from a good length away. You can make up the last few metres to reach them by dropping down and sliding along the turf, with one foot out to kick the ball away. It goes without saying you shouldn't try it on concrete or any other hard surface. Run towards the opponent who has the ball. As you get within striking distance, drop down and slide on one side of your body, with one foot aimed towards the ball and the other leg curled underneath you to slide on. Timing is everything here. If you hit your opponent it's a foul, but if you hit the ball it's a good play. As soon as you slide, jump back up and keep going, even if you miss, so you can carry on chasing your opponent.

WARNING

Never try a sliding tackle from directly behind someone. Not only is it against the rules, but you're likely to hurt them without ever touching the ball. Remember, aim for the ball, not the player, or you'll get sent off.

Jockeying

Tackling is not the only defensive technique in football. 'Jockeying' is another useful skill, where a defending player slows an attacker down by keeping in front of him, blocking a shot on goal, and pushing him away from the danger area in front of the goal. You can't touch an opposing player, but you can get in his way and make it difficult for him to score.

Tackling isn't just for defending players – attackers can also find a well-timed tackle useful to gain possession of the ball close to their opponent's goal-mouth. This can be a crafty way of setting yourself up to score a goal.

If you have the ball and are running to attack the other team's goal, you need to be careful of other players coming to intercept you. Keep the ball close to you rather than kicking it way out in front and running to catch up, and be prepared to change direction quickly to throw off anybody chasing. Finally, if you're trapped by two or more defending players and can't get past without being tackled, look for a teammate who's in a better position and pass the ball to him. Football's a team game, after all, and it's more important that the team gain the lead than that you score the goal yourself.

Training your dog

✤✤✤

Every boy wants to have a faithful canine companion for his best friend. He'll always be there when you need him, even if you leave the poor beast out in the cold and rain for a night. Dogs also love the outdoors, and will tramp with you through snow, icy water, and rough terrain without thinking twice.

Treat your dog with love and he'll repay you with obedience and loyalty. He'll sit and wait for hours for you to come home, and when you're at home, he'll sit by your side and react to your every movement. And once he's got a few tricks and commands under his belt, it won't be long before you're solving crimes and attempting dangerous rescues together.

YOU WILL NEED
- A dog
- A leash
- A toy

Teaching a dog to sit

Every dog should know how to sit. It's the first trick to teach your dog. You may need a number of sessions before he gets the idea, but keep trying.

STEPS

1 FIND A PLACE THAT IS QUIET and free of distractions. Stand in front of your dog and say 'sit' only once (repeating it over and over will train the dog not to listen to your first command).

2 THEN, WITHOUT WAITING to see if the dog will obey, place your dog in the sitting position by pressing on his back end, near the base of his tail.

3 SAY 'GOOD DOG' but don't stroke or touch him in any way. If he gets up, sit him back down while saying 'sit' again. It's important for the dog to remain sitting even through excited conversation.

4 REPEAT THIS PROCESS for about five minutes for each training session.

5 IT'S ALSO IMPORTANT that the dog stay sitting, until you tell him to get up by saying 'OK'. Teach him this by lifting him to a standing position and saying 'OK'.

Teaching a dog to fetch

Most dogs will run and get something when you throw it. Most dogs will also never bring it back. If you want hours of fun in the park with a stick, and your newspaper brought to your feet along with your slippers, fetching is the next thing to teach your dog.

STEPS

1 MAKE SURE THE DOG is on his leash and sitting. Throw his favourite toy a short distance away. Give the command 'fetch' and let him run after the toy while still on his leash.

2 WHEN HE GETS HIS TOY in his mouth, lead him back to you and say 'release'. At the same time offer him a treat and tell him he's a good dog.

3 DO NOT PLAY TUG-OF-WAR with your dog and the toy. That will lead him to think you want to play that game. When given the choice between a treat or a toy, most dogs will drop the toy like a hot potato.

4 ONCE YOUR DOG CAN FETCH, replace the toy with a rolled-up newspaper, saying 'bring the newspaper' as you throw it.

5 AFTER TWO WEEKS OF THIS, take him with you when you fetch the newspaper from the doormat in the morning. Ask him to bring the paper to you. When he does, take the newspaper from him and give him lots of praise and a treat.

6 AFTER ABOUT ANOTHER WEEK, you can ask him to bring the paper while you sit at the breakfast table.

Playing cards: Go Fish

❖ ❖

Climbers on Everest get stuck in snowstorms, and explorers on the Amazon get stuck on sandbars. There are always times on an expedition when you have to sit around and wait for something, and that's why every adventurer should know a good old card game like Go Fish to pass the time.

YOU WILL NEED
- A complete deck of 52 cards
- Between one and nine other players

STEPS

1 IF ONLY TWO PEOPLE ARE PLAYING, deal seven cards to each person. For more than two players, deal out five cards each. Keep the rest of the cards together and place them in the middle of the table.

2 THE YOUNGEST PLAYER STARTS, by asking one other person in the game for a card number to match a card in his or her hand. For example, if you have a two of hearts in your hand, you ask one other player if they have any twos.

3 IF THEY DO, THEY MUST HAND ONE TO YOU. When you get a pair, you lay the pair down in front of you face up and ask again.

4 WHEN YOU ASK FOR A CARD and the person you ask does not have it, they say 'Go fish'. This means you draw one card off the top of the deck. If the card you draw matches a card in your hand, you lay the pair down and ask again. If it does not match any other card in your hand, you keep the card you've picked, but your turn is over and the person on your left gets a turn to ask.

5 THE GAME IS PLAYED UNTIL ALL THE CARDS in the deck have been drawn and all the pairs have been matched. The person with the most pairs wins.

Climbing

꧁ ꧂

No life of adventure will be complete if you don't know how to
scale a tree or a wall. Throw in a bit of rope-climbing, and there's
no obstacle you can't overcome. Scaling the castle walls of the
neighbouring evil sorcerer, or hoisting yourself high up into
the rigging of a pirate ship, will be easy if you master these
simple techniques!

YOU WILL NEED
- A rope slung over a tree branch   • A tree
- A wall

How to climb a rope

1 TO GET STARTED, stand close to the rope so that the bottom end is resting on the
top of your left foot.

2 REACH UP AS HIGH AS YOU CAN and grab hold of the rope with two hands, one
above the other with about a 10-cm (3-in) gap between them.

3 PULL DOWNWARDS, keeping your elbows close to your body while bending the
knees upwards and allowing the rope to stay on the inside arch of your left foot.

4 THEN USE THE BOTTOM OF YOUR RIGHT FOOT to pin the rope against the inside
or top of your left foot. At the same time reach up as high as you can with the
lower hand on the rope and pull downwards, repeating step 3. Keep going until
you reach the top!

5 IF YOU CAN'T GET A GOOD ENOUGH GRIP on the rope with your hands and feet,
tie knots in it about a foot apart and use them as hand- and footholds.

How to climb a wall

1 DEPENDING HOW HIGH A WALL IS, you may be able to get over it without any help. If it's very high, you might try starting from the shoulders of a friend. Sometimes it helps to get a running start and jump to get your hands on the top.

WARNING

Don't jump over a wall if you don't know what's on the other side!

2 EITHER WAY, THE GOAL IS TO JUMP HIGH ENOUGH to get at least one bent elbow on top of the wall. An elbow can support your body better than just your hands. If you can get one elbow up, you can usually work the other elbow up, too, and see what awaits you on the other side.

3 ONCE BOTH ELBOWS ARE ON TOP OF THE WALL, swing one leg up and catch the top of the wall with the inside of your knee.

4 USE YOUR LEG AND ARMS to pull your body up on top of the wall. Sit on the top and have a break after all that effort.

5 ONCE ON TOP, you can lower yourself down the other side in a similar fashion to how you got up, or if it's only a small drop you can just jump.

6 MAKE SURE WHOEVER'S ON THE OTHER SIDE of the wall doesn't mind you climbing over it. You can get in big trouble for trespassing if you're not careful.

How to climb a tree

1 THE BEST TREES TO CLIMB are the ones with lots of low, strong branches. If you're lucky there'll be a strong branch low enough to climb onto, but usually it takes some effort to get to the first branch. To do that, try to jump and grab onto the lowest branch near the base, and brace your feet on the trunk. Then 'walk' up the trunk until you can get a knee over the first branch and swing the rest of your body up.

2 IF THE LOWEST BRANCH IS TOO HIGH to jump up to, try making your way up the trunk by bracing your feet against a nearby rock face, fence, or tree and pushing off the tree you want to climb with your hands. In this way you can 'walk' up the side until you reach a branch.

3 ROPE IS ANOTHER ALTERNATIVE. Tie a bowline loop (see page 13) and toss it over the lowest branch. Or tie a slip knot, and pull the loop tight over the branch. Climb up using the rope-climbing techniques described above.

4 ONCE YOU GET TO THE FIRST BRANCH it's a matter of stepping into the crooks of branches and making your way up. Be sure to keep a good grip with your hands at all times. Trees are excellent spying and look-out points – find a comfortable fork to sit in and watch the world go by.

Epilogue

Now that you've read through the book, it's time to get out there and have some fun! There's a chance you'll feel a little rusty the first few times you climb a tree, fold a paper aeroplane or write a message in invisible ink. But once you get going the fun will come naturally, and you'll wonder what took you so long.

And it gets better. Every adventure is going to be different each time you play, because you'll always find something new. Boys after adventure are like bloodhounds after a scent – we can't stop following it once we find it. And we'll find it sooner or later, if we just turn off the TV, and realise that ordinary back doors can be the gateways to hidden a world of excitement and fun.

Index